DENNIS BURTON 30/3/77

Dennis Burton

Retrospective

The Robert McLaughlin Gallery
Oshawa

Editors:
Meg Hardman
Jennifer Watson
Joan Murray
Dennis Burton

Typesetting:
The Coach House Press

Design:
Carl Brett Design

Printing:
Herzig Sommerville Ltd.

Photograph Credits
Agnes Etherington Art Centre, Queen's University at Kingston
Cat. no. 13

Art Gallery of Ontario, Toronto
Cat. nos. 2, 14, 17, 30, 35, 38

Art Gallery of Ontario, Toronto (McCullach Studio)
Cat. no. 21

Art Gallery of Ontario, Toronto (Ron Vickers)
Cat. no. 15

Ayriss, Toronto
Cat. no. 24

Ian Maceachern, London
Cat. no. 27

The Isaacs Gallery, Toronto (T.E. Moore, Toronto)
Cat. nos. 3, 5, 7, 8, 9, 26, 28, 32, 33, 34, 36, 37, 40, 41, 42

Kitchener-Waterloo Art Gallery
Cat. no. 16

Paul McCarthy, Montreal
Cat. no. 18

The National Gallery of Canada, Ottawa
Cat. nos. 4, 10, 12

Norman Mackenzie Art Gallery, Regina (Brigdens Photo/Graphics Ltd.)
Cat. nos. 19, 20

The Robert McLaughlin Gallery, Oshawa (Peter Richardson)
Cat. nos. 1, 6, 11, 25, 39

Sir George Williams Art Galleries, Concordia University, Montreal
Cat. no. 22

University of Western Ontario, London (Ayriss, Toronto)
Cat. no. 31

The Winnipeg Art Gallery (Ernest Mayer)
Cat. no. 29

Contents

Lenders to the exhibition

Art Gallery of Ontario, Toronto
Mr. & Mrs. L.T. Brouse, Toronto
Walter Carsen, Toronto, and the
    Art Gallery of Hamilton
Irving Grossman, Toronto
Judith and Tom Hendry, Toronto
Mrs. Gail Humphries, Kingston
Indusmin Limited, Toronto
The Isaacs Gallery, Toronto
Mr. & Mrs. Martin Levene, Kitchener
McIntosh Art Gallery,
    University of Western Ontario, London
The National Gallery of Canada, Ottawa
Norman Mackenzie Art Gallery,
    University of Regina, Regina
Mr. & Mrs. David Perlmutter, Toronto
The Robert McLaughlin Gallery, Oshawa
Gordon Sheppard, Montreal
Dr. R.J. Shroyer, London, Ontario
Sir George Williams Art Galleries,
    Concordia University, Montreal
The Winnipeg Art Gallery, Winnipeg
Private collector, Montreal

Exhibition schedule

The Robert McLaughlin Gallery
Oshawa
March 30 – May 1, 1977

Art Gallery of Memorial University of Newfoundland
St. John's
June 20 – July 30, 1977

Beaverbrook Art Gallery
Fredericton
September 8 – October 9, 1977

Southern Alberta Art Gallery
Lethbridge
November 7 – December 4, 1977

The Banff Centre, School of Fine Arts
Banff
January 12 – February 19, 1978

The Saskatoon Gallery and
Conservatory Corporation
Saskatoon
February 27 – March 26, 1978

Art Gallery of Hamilton
Hamilton
April 6 – May 7, 1978

Agnes Etherington Art Centre
Kingston
June 4 – July 9, 1978

Art Gallery of Ontario
Toronto
July 21 – September 3, 1978

Sir George Williams Art Galleries
Concordia University
Montreal
September 14 – October 3, 1978

Acknowledgements

To create this exhibition we have borrowed substantially from eight galleries: Art Gallery of Ontario, Art Gallery of Hamilton, McIntosh Art Gallery (University of Western Ontario), The National Gallery of Canada, Norman Mackenzie Art Gallery (University of Regina), Sir George Williams Art Galleries (Concordia University), and The Winnipeg Art Gallery. Without their cooperation, as well as that of Indusmin Limited, Toronto, we could not have brought this project to realization. The most generous lender to this exhibition is The Isaacs Gallery in Toronto. Avrom Isaacs is Dennis Burton's dealer; his many kindnesses and the generous aid of his assistant, Martha Black, have been invaluable and have shown him in his true light as a friend of contemporary Canadian art.

I would like to thank the Government of Ontario through Wintario for its efforts to help make this catalogue a suitable documentation of this exhibition. The Canada Council, through funding the program at The Robert McLaughlin Gallery, has also assisted in the exhibition.

The collection of The Robert McLaughlin Gallery consists mainly of Painters Eleven (1953-1960) and those artists influenced at the inception of their careers by the work of this group. It is suitable that major purchases of Dennis Burton were made by this gallery in 1976/1977, in the vanguard of the creation of this show.

In organizing the Dennis Burton Retrospective I chose to assist the artist in an autobiographical account of his art. This account constitutes a unique document of painting in the 60s by one of its great verbal exponents, who is also a word painter. We are grateful indeed to the artist for the mammoth amount of time that he took to create this record. We feel that it will form one of the important resources of contemporary Canadian art history.

The staff was particularly involved in the preparations for this exhibition, and I therefore would like to thank them individually: Terry Royle, Cheryl Bromell, Doug MacLean, Gisèle Pageau, Jane Price, Grace Turton, Allan Walkinshaw, Jennifer Watson, and Vicki Michaels who worked on this project during the past summer.

Joan Murray
Director

Dennis Burton

Born Lethbridge, Alberta, 1933. Presently residing in Toronto.
Graduated from the Ontario College of Art with 3 scholarships.
Received the Royal Academy Scholarship 1955.

One-Man Exhibitions
The Gallery of Contemporary Art, Toronto, 1957
The Park Gallery, Toronto, 1959
The Isaacs Gallery, 1962, 1964, 1965, 1968, 1970, 1972, 1976
The Michel Thomas Galleries, Los Angeles, 1962
The New Brunswick Museum, Saint John, 1965
Studio Art Gallery, Vancouver, 1966
McIntosh Memorial Art Gallery, University of Western Ontario,
    London, 1968
Hart House, University of Toronto, 1966
University of Lethbridge, Alberta, 1976

Major Group Exhibitions
Biennial Exhibitions of Canada Painting, The National Gallery
    of Canada, 1957, 1961, 1965, 1968
Four Canadians (Burton, Hodgson, Weisman, Nakamura), Art
    Gallery of Ontario, 1957
Biennial, Walker Art Center, Minneapolis, 1958
Albright-Knox Art Gallery, Buffalo, 1962, 1963, 1964
Winnipeg Biennial Exhibition, Winnipeg Art Gallery, 1962, 1964, 1968
Montreal Museum of Fine Arts, two-man, 1964
Canadian Painting, Memorial Art Gallery of the University of
    Rochester, 1962
2nd Biennial of Canadian Sculpture, The National Gallery of
    Canada, 1963-64
3 plus 1, circulating exhibition through the Art Institute of
    Ontario, 1964-65
Polychrome Construction, The Isaacs Gallery, Toronto, 1965
Outdoor Exhibition, Sculptors' Society of Canada, Stratford, 1965
The Satirical in Art, York University, Toronto, 1966
Survey '70, Montreal Museum of Fine Arts and Art Gallery of
    Ontario, 1970
Toronto Painting: 1953-1965, The National Gallery of Canada
    and Art Gallery of Ontario, 1972
Contemporary Ontario Art, opening show of the Art Gallery of
    Ontario, 1974
1st Dalhousie Drawing Exhibition, Dalhousie University Art
    Gallery, Halifax, 1976
Ontario Now, Art Gallery of Hamilton and Kitchener-Waterloo
    Art Gallery, 1975
Celebration of the Body, Agnes Etherington Art Centre,
    Queen's University at Kingston, 1976
The Ontario Community Collects, Art Gallery of Ontario, 1975-76
Abstractions, Province of Ontario exhibition at the Olympic
    Games, Montreal, 1976

Awards and Commissions
Walker Art Center Biennial, 1958: three prizes
Windmill Point Canadian Painting Competition, Ile Perrot,
    Montreal, 1959: first prize
Granby International, 1959: first prize
Western Ontario Annual Exhibition, 1959: first prize, painters
    under 30 years
11th Winnipeg Show, 1968: first prize painting
Canada Council Fellowships, 1961, 1968-69, 1969-70,
    1972-73, 1975-76
Commissioned for mural, residence Mr. & Mrs. J.D. Eaton,
    1962
Commissioned for mural, Edmonton International Airport,
    1963
Commissioned to design postage stamp, honouring Henry
    Kelsey, 1969

Represented in the Collections of:
Art Bank, The Canada Council, Ottawa
Art Gallery of Ontario, Toronto
Art Gallery of Windsor
Canadian Imperial Bank of Commerce, Toronto
Crown Life Insurance Company, Toronto
Department of External Affairs, Ottawa
The Edmonton Art Gallery
Estate of Charles Laughton, Hollywood, California
Gulf Minerals of Canada, Toronto
Hart House, University of Toronto
Imperial Oil Limited, Toronto
Los Angeles County Museum of Art
McIntosh Memorial Art Gallery, University of Western Ontario,
    London
The Metropolitan Museum of Art, New York
Montreal Museum of Fine Arts
Mount Allison University, Sackville
The National Gallery of Canada, Ottawa
The New Brunswick Museum, Saint John
Norman Mackenzie Art Gallery, University of Regina
Pasadena Museum of Modern Art, California
The Robert McLaughlin Gallery, Oshawa
Sir George Williams Art Galleries, Concordia University,
    Montreal
Smithsonian Institution, Washington
University of British Columbia, Vancouver
University of Waterloo
Walker Art Center, Minneapolis, Minnesota
The Winnipeg Art Gallery

Beginnings (1933-1952)

Fig. 1 Dennis Burton's father with his dance band, The Ambassadors, at Lethbridge Henderson Lake Pavilion, 1942.

My father was born near Brandon, Manitoba, and had several brothers and sisters. His name was Clarence Edward Frederic Burton but he was called Eddie. He could repair automobiles, electrical appliances, musical instruments and other mechanical things and make anything at all out of wood, metal, plastic, or aluminum, including his own tools. As a child I hung around his workshop on weekends and I remember how very fastidious and orderly he was, preferring to be in his garage workshop than to be in the house or at his various employments. He had every sort of tool from planes and sanders to all sizes of nails and screws which he kept in cigarette tins, each clearly marked with whatever was in it. My father loved music and taught himself how to play the clarinet and all three types of saxophones while he was working for a musical instrument store in Lethbridge; he played saxophone in various dixie and dance bands of his own and he played drums for silent movies (Fig. 1).

During the Depression, my father sold men's clothing door to door and I remember his sample suitcases, like Marcel Duchamp's *Valise*. In them were half items such as one shoe or half a shirt, from which customers could order. During the war he was an insurance salesman. The major part of his job was insuring Commonwealth airmen and he used to go out to No. 8 Bombing and Gunnery School at Lethbridge Airport and sell insurance to the gunners and bombardiers who didn't have any, so that, if they were killed, their wives and children would have some money. When he died, at age fifty-five, the funeral was an extremely large one for Lethbridge because everybody knew Eddie and knew that he wanted to help people. His life has been a guiding light for me.

My Dad always had copies of magazines like *Mechanics Illustrated* and *Popular Science,* and I, of course, used to read them too. They had a page in them about things of the future such as flying wings, mono-rail trains, trips to other planets — fantastic scientific stuff which I loved to look at. He collected the 'Pulps' like *Astounding Science-Fiction* and *Planet Stories, Amazing Stories* and *Wonder Stories* published 1926-1936, where I first saw the black and white scratchboard illustrations of Virgil Finlay. Like most boys, from 1936 through 1949, I had a treasured collection of comic books: *Superman, Captain Marvel, Batman* (1939), *Captain America, Hawkman, Blackhawk, Airboy, The Spirit;* my favourites were *Wings Comics, Jungle Comics* and *Planet Comics.*

'Flash Gordon', 'Brick Bradford' and 'Buck Rogers' were newspaper daily strips I followed. Burne Hogarth was drawing 'Tarzan' which *The Star Weekly* carried. I thought comic book and comic strip art was THE ONLY ART. I made several strips of my own.

Dad used to encourage me to make things and, in my pre-high school years, I kept busy making balsa wood models of the major airplanes of World War II and collecting the three-viewpoint line drawings of airplanes on the backs of Sweet Caporal cigarette packages. I taught myself to draw my favorite fighters: Spitfires, P-51 Mustangs, Zeros and Stukas.

Dad was interested in art in a very unusual way, and this has much to do with sexual art and artistic sex. He had a scrapbook in which, in his bachelor days, he had stuck every picture of a nude woman that he would have found available at that time: no dirty postcards, nothing pornographic, just sepia ink and photographic reproductions of second and third rate romantic sexual paintings by middle and late nineteenth cen-

Fig. 2 Milton Caniff cartoon-strip,
Terry and the Pirates,
1947

tury French academic artists, and nudes by Rubens, Courbet, Bouguereau and Titian. None of these nudes had pubic hair. The scrapbook was always hidden away so that I couldn't see them. By about 1940, he had collaged over and covered up all these sexually inspirational pictures, with maps and head-lines about the war. But underneath were the pictures of scan-tily clad, luscious ladies. When my parents went out on a Saturday night and I was left alone, I used to take this scrap-book out of an old steamer trunk in the porch, and look under-neath the war pictures to see those sexy pictures and I used to get horny. When I was about eight years old I also disco-vered at the bottom of the trunk a two-inch thick book all about sex; in it were items about mandrake roots looking like sexual objects, and Egyptian art showing the god Osiris with an erection. There were sexual diagrams and graphic pictures of vulvas and penises and medical anatomy drawings. I used to sneak a look as soon as my parents left the house – my curiosity about sex was insatiable. All these pictures were sources of erotic stimulation, as were the photos and draw-ings of women in underclothes in the Eaton's and Simpson's catalogues and the ads for bras and girdles in American women's magazines.

My mother, Bertha, was born into the Tiller family of two brothers and one sister. Her parents came west from New-foundland before 1910. My grandfather was a carpenter. He died in 1972 aged 100 years. My mother has always encour-aged my art. She supported my father and me by working as assistant manager of a stationery store in Lethbridge, 1940 through '65. From it she bought art supplies for me. She has always helped me spiritually and financially.

My mother and my father were naturally creative. I had always shown a strong interest in drawing, and in public school I was generally given a lot of encouragement by my various teachers. I used to decorate the blackboards at Hallowe'en, Christmas and other holidays, staying in after four to brighten up the boards with coloured chalk drawings of burning candles and poinsettias for Christmas, hearts for St. Valentine's Day, four-leaf clovers for St. Patrick's Day and bunny rabbits and eggs for Easter. I was a one-man greeting-card factory. Most of my teachers in public school and high school through grade 11 encouraged my art work. Good psychology for those days – they would rather have my art on the blackboards and in an accessible and expressed form than in my school workbooks, the margins and back-pages of which were filled anyway with imitations of Milton Caniff adventure comic strip characters.

I had closely followed Caniff's 'Terry and the Pirates' until it ended in December 1947, and then the new strip 'Steve Can-yon' up until 1952 (Fig. 2). My other favourite artist was Alex Raymond who created 'Flash Gordon' and drew the detective strip 'Rip Kirby'. Huntley Brown was also interested in Milton Caniff and Alex Raymond, and we used to get together and

3 Monarch 1958
Oil on masonite
48 x 48 in.
The Isaacs Gallery, Toronto

5 Serves Me Right (Anvil) 1959
Oil on masonite
48 x 60 in.
The Isaacs Gallery, Toronto

try to draw like them. These comic strip artists were very important to me. In Alberta then, except for the Simpson's and Eaton's catalogues, American women's magazines, *The Star Weekly* and the Sunday funnies, there was no visual culture. There was only one art book in the public library. In it I saw Michelangelo's Libyan Sibyl drawing; I dearly wanted to draw like that.

From 1944 to 1950, I was very interested in editorial illustration such as what appeared in American women's magazines like *Ladies' Home Journal, Good Housekeeping, Redbook, Colliers', The Saturday Evening Post* and the magazines my mother and dad bought after the Second World War. I never read the novels or looked at the ads (except for bra and girdle ads), but I did look at the illustrations by the artists who later formed the Famous Artists course for students wanting to study illustration, correspondence-style. My favourite was Robert Fawcett.

From 1947 to '50, I took the 'draw me' correspondence course from Art Instruction Inc. in Minneapolis, studying perspective, tone, brush drawing, etc., so I had learned all those things at the age of fourteen, fifteen, sixteen, several years before I went to the Ontario College of Art. I did eleven of the twelve divisions and got pretty good marks, B+ and A's. My instructor was Charles Schulz who later went on to be the creator of 'Peanuts'. Going to Pickering College in Ontario in 1950 interrupted that course; I remember taking the books with me but I never got back to it, I had too much homework. I did grades 12 and 13 at Pickering, passing nine subjects by June 1952. I was eighteen years old.

While in grades 10 and 11, I had been working in a Lethbridge framing store after school and on Saturdays. I framed some of Roloff Beny's prints, and his semi-abstract drawings of the figure inspired me. I also framed hundreds of those amateurish heavily textured landscape paintings so I got interested in painting, but drawing and inking comic strips was still my major preoccupation.

During the same period I also became very interested in bebop and modern jazz and played drums in an orchestra

9

called 'The Collegians'. At first, I was playing only Saturday nights, then later – three nights a week at the The Pavilion in Lethbridge, and practising all day Sundays. It was great! I was a pro Gene Krupa or Buddy Rich at the age of fourteen, sweat and all. But my marks in high school suffered because of the late nights, 'the entertainer's life' (the alcohol, Chinese food at 3 or 4 a.m., the girls etc.) so my Mom and Dad urged me to quit, which I did in 1949. I passed my grade 11 with honours in several subjects, including chemistry. The guidance teacher gave us an assignment to write 'what we wanted to do when we grew up'; I submitted a thick book about wanting to be a commercial artist and got a very high mark.

In 1950, I applied for a scholarship sponsored by the Lethbridge 'Old Boys Association' of Pickering College (advertised in the *Lethbridge Herald*) worth one thousand dollars, to attend Pickering College in Newmarket, Ontario. On July 1st, I was announced the winner, and so in September 1950 I came east to go to this boys' private school to get my senior matriculation.

The head master of Pickering College at that time, Robert E.K. Rourke, was a collector of the Group of Seven and the later Canadian Group of Painters. In the halls of the school and in the dining room were paintings by Franz Johnston, A.Y. Jackson, Arthur Lismer, A.J. Casson, J.E.H. MacDonald, Will Ogilvie and Jock Macdonald. Seeing these paintings every day, I soon developed preferences. Why do so many people put Franz Johnston down? For me he was the best inventive technician of the Group. There were few Tom Thomsons in Rourke's collection, but that didn't matter. The paintings at Pickering really impressed me, especially their surfaces and textures, but after seeing all those landscapes of northern Ontario I knew I didn't want to do that kind of art. I was not interested in landscape, nor in figurative painting; I was still interested in comic strips. Enclosed in the weekly letter from home were the five daily strips of 'Steve Canyon' and 'Rip Kirby' and the *Star Weekly* colour page of 'Steve Canyon', which my father faithfully clipped out every day for five years.

Fred Hagan's influence on me began during my two years at Pickering College and it was through him that I came to know Michael Snow, Dick Williams and Graham Coughtry even before I started at the Ontario College of Art. Fred lived in Newmarket, where Pickering College is, and did the stage

sets for the plays and the Gilbert and Sullivan operettas that Bob Rourke presented each year. I was picked to be Hagan's assistant, and it was while painting flats that I painted on stretched canvas for the first time. I often babysat for Fred Hagan and his wife, Isabelle, and I would look at his work. Fred's influence was in the direction of the German Northern Gothic Renaissance. I felt that way at the time – distorted. I was going through an identity crisis sexually and physically during my last year at Pickering.

Art School and Early Influences (1952-1956)

I attended the Ontario College of Art from 1952 to 1956. After the first year foundation course; I took the drawing and painting course instead of the advertising art course. In foundation year, the commercial art that was part of that course involved imitating lettering with certain kinds of speedball pens etc., and I wasn't too good at that. I also had trouble measuring with a ruler, probably due to my disgust for geometry and arithmetic, thanks to a teacher I had in grade 3 who was a real bitch and who once demonstrated how to use an eraser to the class by rubbing my arm until it bled to show the kids how not to rub out with an ink eraser. At least she taught me how to use an eraser so you don't rip the paper.

I didn't do very well in the design and lettering stuff and I can remember the principal, Sidney Watson, meeting us individually after the foundation year and asking, 'What do you want to do now?' He was supposed to advise us and I said I wanted to go into the advertising art course because I had always wanted to be a comic strip artist and illustrator. He said, 'You'll never make it, so I suggest you go into drawing and painting.' (In 1952 I saw the film *An American in Paris* shortly after it was released — and the story about an American painter in Paris, and Gershwin's music, convinced me that what I wanted to be was a painter.) But I am content that Watson suggested it.

When I was in my first year, Graham Coughtry and John Meredith were in fourth year and I used to admire and respect them because they would come into a life class where we'd all be doing this OCA style of drawing and they would just sit down at the drawing board with expensive paper and a charcoal pencil and do these Ben Shahn-like, quick, incredible drawings. I used to stand there in awe at their facility.

For my second year I was in the painting department and my teacher for still life and oil painting was Jock Macdonald. He was the only person I could talk to on the faculty, except for Fred Hagan whom I already knew. I tried talking to Jack Nichols, Will Ogilvie, Eric Freifeld, John Alfsen, Carl Schaefer and a few others about illustration, comic strip inking, and modern painting but they didn't talk much, whereas Jock did; he wanted to communicate. He did not get along with the rest of the staff; they ostracized him; it was a ridiculous situation. Jock didn't like his classes to be too serious so I brought in a portable record player and I used to play bebop and modern jazz 10" LPs. He encouraged me to do free abstractions.

Often when I came in late I would have to paint on the model stand because there was no room, so I would sit up there and do my own abstract paintings while the rest of the class were painting still life objects. I never thought at the time about being self-conscious, just accepted that I had to sit there, but I realize now it was a kind of method and technique demonstration I was doing, because gradually over the next two years before I graduated, just about everybody in that class had started to shift towards abstraction. It is significant that during my years 1952 to '56 at OCA the entire period was 'The McCarthy Era' in the USA. I found the general political philosophy at OCA to be one linked with exactly what Senator McCarthy was attempting to purge in U.S. Government. I sought a kind of painting unencumbered by politics. I found abstract expressionism — it was 'free'!

Milton Caniff came to Toronto when I was in my third year at OCA. I met him and showed him all the strips I had made, and he said, 'Look Dennis, your imitations of what I do are terrific, but you go your way, you are studying to be a painter and you will be happier in that than in trying to imitate me. The comic strip business is terrible, the deadlines are awful! I advise you not to get into it, don't even try, but you know, Dennis, I have never seen anybody who can draw as much like myself as you can!' Having met Caniff, the idol dissolved in front of me and I lost interest in doing comic strips and took his advice seriously.

The Lebrun anatomical-distortion influence that had started with Fred Hagan in 1952, while I was at Pickering College, came to a conclusion in 1955. I was in my third year at OCA when I got an anonymous $500 travelling scholarship to go to California to study with Rico Lebrun. (I still don't know where the money came from.) I studied with Lebrun during the summer between my third and fourth years, and also with Francis de Erdeley at U.S.C., Los Angeles. Lebrun was an excellent draughtsman, so that when coming back to OCA for my last year I had been through a whole new educational system that was very, very demanding and different from OCA. Lebrun made us learn to draw the figure in two or three different ways; he called it 'conceptual drawing' — one exercise was to have the model come in and stand for five minutes and then leave, and for us to draw what we had seen as accurately as possible, from memory! Another exercise was to draw the figure's rear from the front view, or vice versa,

8 Burlesque Case 1960
Oil on plywood
52 3/4 x 52 3/4 in.
The Isaacs Gallery, Toronto

14 False-True 1962
Oil on canvas
60 x 60 in.
Renée and David Perlmutter, Toronto

having never seen the model before. If we were drawing a flower (it sounds very much like Actors' Studio and other concepts about acting and writing, etc.) we were *to be the flower,* in order to understand how to draw it. They were marvellous ideas, and when I went back to OCA I started working this way, and it was about this time the teachers decided not to mark my work because they 'did not understand it', had never seen anything like it before, and it didn't conform to what they wanted. Strangely enough, the year after I left I heard from guys like Bob Markle and Rick Gorman and others who were two years behind me at OCA that those drawing teachers had shifted over to this 'conceptual drawing' and they were teaching all the things I had learned in California – incredible!

Under the Lebrun influence I did a lot of paintings about jazz musicians. At Christmas '55, I won the Royal Academy Scholarship for OCA tying for first place with Edmund Alleyn. I

got $400, a drawing was reproduced in *The Globe and Mail* and it was the first time I had been applauded for my 'fine art' work. Those works were the final Lebrun-influenced stuff I did.

At the beginning of my fourth year at OCA, Gord Rayner, Bob Smith and I moved into a place on Charles Street East in Toronto where the post office is now, called the Villa Crispin. It was an old run-down house and the landlord, Mr. Charman, let us have the top floor for a very cheap rent. Between September and Christmas, a Painters Eleven show came to Hart House, University of Toronto, and Gord and I went to see it, arriving just before it closed. For the first time we saw huge paintings by Ronald, Cahén, Town, Bush, Nakamura, Luke, Gordon, Yarwood, Mead, Hodgson and Jock Macdonald. Gord and I were unbelievably stimulated by these totally abstract works. I was aware at this point of Motherwell and De Kooning and Abstract Expressionism from reading *Art News*

17 Bay-Yonge-Bloor 1963
Oil on canvas
84 x 60 in.
Renée and David Perlmutter, Toronto

24 Egypt Asleep 1966
Oil on canvas
60 x 60 1/8 in.
Walter Carsen, Toronto

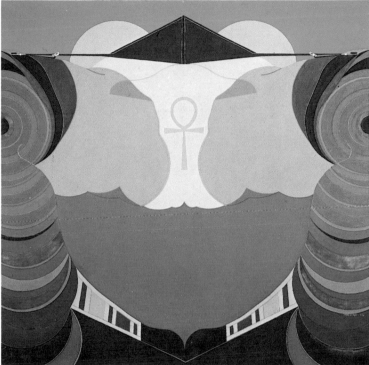

ings that same day, and vowed over some Hudson's Bay rum never to paint representationally again! We both felt 're-leased' but were nonetheless a little doubtful whether what we had produced was really and honestly what the Painters Eleven paintings were all about. Our first attempts were reactions; both of us discovered innate, child-like originality which had been dormant. It was electrifying!

We started working this way and in November we wanted some kind of criticism. York Wilson and Cleve Horne came to see my work; Wilson had been sent a letter about me from Lebrun. Rico had said York was the most important artist in Canada, and that he should help me after the summer. So Wilson and Horne came over to our studio and saw our abstractions. They thought we were doing terrific things and they told us about how tough art was. They said nothing terribly critical; we felt pretty good. I remember the day Graham

but had never seen their paintings 'live'. We just couldn't conceive of painting with such strength and power, all purely abstract but not like Mondrian, or Picasso, or Kandinsky. Such surfaces! Gord and I went back to our studio that Sunday and painted our first non-objective, non-figurative abstract paint-

Coughtry and Mike Snow came over to see what we were doing and I never knew why they came or who invited them, but we really had a good time that day, because they 'knew what was happening' and were impressed by our paintings. At a party last year I said to Graham, 'You know, back in the fall of '55 you and Mike came over one day to our studio to see what we were doing. Why did you guys come over?' and his answer was, 'We were trying to find out if anybody was having more fun than we were.' Graham hasn't changed since 1955 — he's still looking for, and finding, more 'fun' than anybody else I know.

That Painters Eleven show at Hart House changed my point of view entirely, so from November '55 on, I concentrated on abstraction. I can remember when John Meredith came to visit me in February '56. (I was living on the third floor of the 'House of Hambourg' studio on Cumberland Street, Toronto's only underground jazz club where local musicians played.) I knew he had been at OCA at the same time as Coughtry but I didn't know his work at all. When he came over to see me I had just finished *Jeruvia* (Pl.2), and he said, 'That is the same painting I just did!' so then I knew that Meredith was 'into the same thing'. In fact he had been painting totally abstractly for years! That was also the day he told me he was Bill Ronald's brother, which simply 'floored' me. We became good friends; it felt good to know that I was amidst painters who thought as I did, as opposed to my OCA classmates who laughed at abstract art.

In March 1956, though still at OCA, I had a show at the House of Hambourg (my first one-man show which I put up myself). Most of the paintings in the show were totally abstract, some were early figurative with the Lebrun influence. I sold five to various jazz fans. I was becoming my own version of the painter in *An American in Paris* — I was 'An Albertan in Toronto', still searching for my 'Leslie Caron'.

In late March of my fourth year, I wanted to know how I was doing so one day I went into Carl Schaefer's office (he had taken over as head of the painting department when George Pepper died in 1955) and saw that my marks were in 'C' category. I was furious so I wrote a long, blistering letter to the painting department, pointing out that my performance over the four years had been better than that of anybody in my class; that I had won scholarships in drawing and painting at the end of the second and third years; that I had performed exactly as required throughout the four years until the latter half of the final year in terms of meeting the academic requirements; that because the teachers refused to give me marks in the last few months was no reason not to consider the high marks I had achieved previously. (Being president of the Students' Council had its drawbacks, I was just too busy with too much: doing my own work, attending classes, managing the Council, having exhibitions, running the coffee and sandwich concession at OCA, working at the Jazz Club and presenting jazz concerts at OCA.) So they had a meeting and put me where I belonged which was about fourth from the top, though actually I should have been first, even with the extra-curricular activities. I had wanted to compete for the travelling scholarship but the choice of people to be in the juried exhibition had already been made prior to my marks being changed. I accepted that but still thought I should have an exhibition of my work; so I set up my own in an empty second floor OCA painting studio with the help of the janitor; we hung some fifty things I had done In and out of class, knowing that the jury would see them even though they couldn't consider my work as part of the competition.

Jock Macdonald, who had been away in Europe on a sabbatical, came back for graduation in time to see my exhibition. He told my parents, who came for the graduation in May '56, that regardless of my final marks, I was the best painter he had encountered since Bill Ronald and that I should be encouraged to continue painting. He said I had 'it'.

In 1955, before Jock went to Europe, he had submitted my name for the Guggenheim competition. I didn't find out however until 1957 when I found the invitation where it had fallen down behind the radiator upon which the mail was placed at the Charles Street studio. So I didn't know that I had been invited to compete for a Guggenheim scholarship in '56, the same year Ronald and Coughtry did.

In the last year at OCA my work had somehow managed to attract the attention of Shirley Driver of the Art Gallery of Toronto, with the result that she included my work in her 1957 show called 'Four Canadians' — the others were Tom Hodgson, Kazuo Nakamura and Gus Weisman. It was a great honour for me to be in their company and it was the first feather in my cap. I was 'launched'! It was 'Go for broke'!

In about 1960, I thought I would find out what had happened to the people I went to school with. Eighty people started with me in the foundation year; about twenty in second year (the first year of the drawing and painting course) and by the time we were in fourth year there were eighteen left. By 1960, I was the only one still painting as their 'life-work'.

I had worked my way through Pickering College and OCA by working summers as a labourer back home in Alberta. I worked in a dairy, as a picture framer, and on aluminum sprinkler systems for irrigation. I had a lot of financial help from my parents, even though we were lower middle class. When I got out of art school I didn't have any money; I had used it all up for tuition, materials, rent and all that stuff. I walked around the streets trying to find a job, figuring that my skill and diploma were going to get me some work — because you can't eat eggshells, you know — and I was really quite upset when I couldn't find anything in any advertising agency or any commercial areas of illustration — just nothing. I finally took a job that was from midnight to eight o'clock in the morning at Union Station in Toronto in the CPR on IBM computers, the first in Canada, keeping track of freight train consorts between the east and west sides of the Ontario district. Working with me on that night shift were another artist and a guy who was going in for medicine. The three of us used to listen to jazz on the radio and we had a great time. I quit after six months because I was trying to keep an impossible kind of schedule. I'd go home at eight and, because it was morning and everybody else was getting up and all the vibrations of going to work were happening, I'd stay up and paint until around five in the afternoon, and then try to get a few hours sleep before going in at midnight. I found that because of lack of sleep and lack of eating, I used to sit there and look at the digital clock-type transceiver concentratedly and watch the one turn into a two and three, and I'd think, I'm going to make a film about this, but I used to hypnotize myself watching it and I remember one night waking screaming because the numbers were in a nightmare and were no longer numbers but very threatening geometric images.

It was Graham Coughtry who in January/February '57 suggested that I come to the graphic design department at the CBC and see David Mackay, the art director there. I remember what I did to impress David Mackay; I took perhaps fifty or sixty photographs of important persons from copies of *Time* and drew likenesses with brush and ink, sometimes with pen and ink, in little vignettes which I took in to show him. He was impressed by my style and my calligraphy and the way I could draw faces exactly as they looked. I was hired as a senior graphic designer. This meant that I didn't have to 'apprentice'. I stayed with the CBC three years (February 1957 — October

28 Yonique Metaphor – Prismadame 1967
Oil on canvas
60 x 60 in.
The Isaacs Gallery, Toronto

29 Niagara Rainbow Honeymoon No. 1 – The Bedroom 1967-68
Oil on canvas
60 x 60 in.
The Winnipeg Art Gallery
Donated by the Women's Committee, 1968

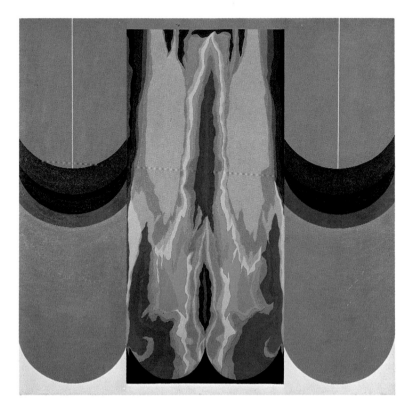

1960). I illustrated children's stories for television and I did promo cards and graphic stills to illustrate news items. That was at the time when typography in commercial art had suddenly come from nowhere and become the major style of advertising. It was like the use of typography as an end in itself rather than a means to an end. Allan Fleming of course, of Cooper & Beatty, was away ahead of everybody in using type design, and it was he who taught me principles of typography while I was at CBC. Some of the guys I had gone to OCA with were working at Cooper & Beatty and other type houses in Toronto and they also were into this avant garde type of design. I loved typography, it was like playing with painting images – the nightmare became a reality I could control.

In 1957 came the most important 'turn-on'. Gord Rayner and Ross Mendes took me to see the new permanent collection at the Albright-Knox Gallery in Buffalo. Now, the AGO (the

Art Gallery of Toronto at that point) had not yet bought any of the modern Americans or modern Europeans – there were no Klines, no De Koonings, no Rothkos to see – but the Albright-Knox had a marvellous permanent collection and I just can't remember how many weekends we went down to Buffalo to see works by De Kooning, Rothko, Clyfford Still, Kenzo Okada and many other artists whom we all had been digging as a result of reading the U.S. art magazines. I can remember standing in front of De Kooning's *Gotham News* for the first time. The experience is indelibly etched in my mind. Having had all that conservative academic training at OCA, I said 'You can't do that! You can't break up charcoal like that in the paint film, you can't put paint on like that!' It was a complete antithesis and antagonistic to the way I'd been trained. I couldn't stand it! It made me want to paint. It was an erotic experience. Back in Toronto, we went to our studios and started our first New York influenced abstractions.

38 Up-Tight News 1974
Acrylic on canvas
64 1/8 x 47 1/8 in.
Indusmin Limited, Toronto

42 Coming Down 1976
Acrylic on canvas
72 x 90 in.
The Isaacs Gallery, Toronto

I had occasion to go to New York with my first wife at Christmas 1957 and saw in various galleries and museums the work of Joan Mitchell, Nicolas Carone, Nicolas Calas, Adja Junkers, John Grillo, Helen Frankenthaler, Ralph Humphrey, Paul Jenkins, Grace Hartigan, Stephen Green, Michael Goldberg, John Ferren, Nassos Daphnis, James Brooks, Marca-Relli and a lot of other painters who really impressed me, especially Alfred Leslie and the younger New York school painters like Norman Bluhm. I came back to Toronto and started to work more firmly in that direction.

I had a studio for the first time alone about August 1957 on Bedford Road. There I did paintings like *December Red, Can-Can* and *Jordu.* My father died quite unexpectedly on October 6th, 1957. His dying affected me dramatically; I

came back to Toronto driving his old Studebaker and vowed that I was going to 'make it' in honour of my father — make a name for myself, as good as the name he had left in my home town. Back in Toronto, I really got involved with painting and looking after my job at the CBC. I did the painting *October 6, 1957* then, in honour of my father's death. I entered the Windmill Point Competition (at Ile Perrot, P.Q.) and won second prize. I entered the Monsanto Competition and had an Honourable Mention. A few things I had done for the graphic design department of CBC were published in *Canadian Art.* I was becoming known through shipping my paintings to all kinds of exhibitions, from Newfoundland to Vancouver.

In the fall of '58, I started to work on my own abstract style. I felt a stronger influence from New York, from artists like Twarkov and especially De Kooning. *Monarch* was painted about this time (Pl. 3). It was the fourth or fifth major 4' x 4' abstraction that I did on masonite. Some of the elements in it were based on photographs which I took of my father's basement workshop in the house on 14th Street in Lethbridge, which explains why *Monarch* has an image in it, in the lower left corner, of an air compressor my father had made from the wing tank of an airplane and to which he attached a motor so he could spray paint. The other abstract shapes and images I can't explain, other than that they were the right shapes for the painting at the time. *Monarch* has to do not only with the Monarch Hill near Lethbridge but also with 'monarch' in the sense of a king, which is how I had thought of my father.

In September '58 I moved my studio to 16 Huntley Street and prepared for a show of my work which was to be held at the Park Gallery on Avenue Road. It was THE gallery for Painters Eleven: Harold Town showed there, as did Oscar Cahén, Tom Hodgson, Walter Yarwood etc. That gallery 'took me on' after the Gallery of Contemporary Art became defunct in the summer of '58. The show included paintings and small and large metal sculptures, and was held in February/March 1959. It was reviewed by Robert Fulford in *The Toronto Star* in the same columns as the review of Joyce Wieland's and Gord Rayner's two-man show at The Isaacs Gallery.

In May '59, I won the Granby International Painting Competition, defeating Harold Town and many other artists from Canada and Europe. I then decided to go to Maine to study at the Skowhegan School of Painting and Sculpture. While I was there, in July and August '59, I met Ben Shahn who urged me to leave commercial art and paint, paint, paint. In the summer of '60, while out West, I became so determined to concentrate only on painting that I decided to quit my job at the CBC.

I resigned from my graphic designer job at the CBC in October 1960. At the same time I left my first wife Donna (Fig. 4), which gave me a sense of freedom, and I moved in to the studio at 45 Wellesley Street East. I was 'on edge', because I had to prepare for my first one-man show at The Isaacs Gallery in January 1961.

Around the middle of September '60 I did *The Game of Life,* 54″ x 84″, the largest painting I had ever done (Pl. 12). This work was motivated by an African sculpture show at The Isaacs Gallery. I feel that the painting reflects the impact of primitive sculpture on me, in the same way that sculpture, African sculpture, affected Picasso and led him to Cubism. I started painting images of genitalia very obviously for the first time in *Smokeshop Sex Marauder* (Pl. 9). In *The Game of Life,* the painting of the breasts, the mouths and teeth, and the area where I put my hands and palm marks, were a response to primitive art. Those variations on penis and testicle shapes (Joyce Wieland used these in *Nature Mixes,* 1963, her painting about a hand turning into a flower, then into a penis) broke through my inhibitions, personally and socially. *The Game of Life* painting was a fight against facility by making a very loose, almost childlike work.

That canvas was followed by another of the same size, a large grey painting influenced by Barnett Newman and called *Banana Split* (it has since been destroyed). I also did *Electric Light Train to Ecru City, Sagittarius* and *Shadows Landing* around that time, and *Stitt* which was renamed *Around the World.* This painting was in the Spring '61 show at the Montreal Museum of Fine Arts and it was there that Charles Laughton the actor became interested in my work.

In December 1960 Jock Macdonald died. This was a terrible loss. Since I was working on my show, his death gave me a new reason to go on, but it was disappointing that Jock would never see it. In that show I exhibited my recently finished *The Game of Life* (P. 12), *Flame Birth, Electric Light Train to Ecru City, Diagram — Portrait Reflection of Myself, Exodus, Sagittarius, Stitt, Smokeshop Sex Marauder* (Pl. 9) as well as a few combines and dada objects that I had made.

Life was really tough after I quit the CBC. I was heavily in debt to the tune of $3,000 or more, and was counting on the show at Isaacs to bring in some money, but nothing sold! Nothing, that is, until April '61 when Charles Laughton visited me and bought several paintings and drawings. Later that

Fig. 4 The Burtons, Dennis, Donna Miller,
Donna's daughter,
in Bermuda, Christmas, 1957

year I sent him slides of my work and these he showed to several influential people in California who eventually bought fifteen or so works.

Mike Snow and Joyce Wieland wanted to do a show of erotic art and came over to my studio early in '61 to see if I had more things like *Stitt* and *The Game of Life,* but I had nothing terribly explicit. The one most indicative of what I'd be getting into later around 1965 was *Smokeshop Sex Marauder* of 1960 (Pl. 9). Most people misread that painting and thought it was anything but the actual subject. Though intended as a

middle-class value shock, then, in 1960, they didn't recognize the imagery which was a close-up on panties over genitals with a lot of pink texture suggesting very frilly, lacy, bikini panties. On each side, left and right, there was a garter strap coming down. At that point I hadn't really studied the construction of garters so didn't paint the mechanism very well. I didn't really depict the garter construction properly until I began the 1964-65 paintings when I drew the garters according to the way they were engineered. *Smokeshop Sex Marauder* was abstract expressionist in execution, so that photo-realistic garters were out.

In May I heard that I'd been awarded a $2,000 Canada Council Grant. Gord Rayner and Graham Coughtry also received grants that year, and we were the only younger artists to get them. It had been a tough winter financially, but eventually I paid all my debts, thanks to the Laughton purchases and the Canada Council Grant. I had lost weight and was exhausted, and I'd really had enough of Toronto, so in June I drove a second-hand agency U-drive car out to my mother's in Alberta and stayed there for a rest until September.

I got back to Toronto in September '61 and made a trip to New York City the following month. I saw the first Morris Louis show of vertical stripes (the candy stripe paintings) at the André Emmerich Gallery and I remember writing two paragraphs in the guest book saying how I thought this was the greatest thing I'd ever seen. This was one of my major turnons, the other being my first De Kooning at the Albright-Knox.

After the New York trip I did *Before Goldberg* and *Brick of the Month* (Pl. 13), the latter being based on images in a manual of sexual anatomy I'd bought, and also on an incredible sexual experience I'd had in New York. The title *Brick of the Month* was later changed to *Neapolitan* because it has the colours of strawberry, chocolate and vanilla ice cream. There are a lot of condensed De Kooning shapes in that painting.

At a New Year's Eve party I met my next wife, Heather. I did several good portrait drawings of her because she had a beautiful face. During '62 I did paintings like *Biologic* and *Blue Bird Pas de Deux,* most of them on square canvas and subtly based on female subject matter. I started doing some drawings too, of Heather seated with her skirt up, showing thighs, stockings and garterbelt or tights. But I didn't 'zoom in' on the subject exclusively.

I was commissioned to paint a mural at the home of Mrs. John David Eaton, on a curved wall in the recreation room. On March 20th Heather had a positive pregnancy test. I couldn't get a decree absolute from my first wife, but Heather was living with me and I painted that mural with the stress and tension of knowing I was going to have my first child. It was a beautiful thing, 5' x 15', and I painted it in three days – March 20th – 22nd.

Though I continued to paint, after March things became terrible. I had few painting sales, no commercial art jobs and, after waiting all summer, only two works were sold from a show I had in California. Apart from $10 a week from Av Isaacs, we had no cash, no food and I was worried about Heather and the unborn child. It was in that period that I did *False-True* (Pl. 14), a mirror image painting with one side reflecting the other, but not exactly. It's a distorted reflection of the imagery down at the lower right that reflects over to the left, and vice versa. It was the second time I had used a large field of colour (the first time being in the painting *Matador*). In that same period I did *Gallery* for which I used up all available paint – pastels, house paint, everything.

On the advice of my insurance agent I cashed in my life policy. Also through him we found a better place to live, a house on Erskine Avenue into which we moved in September. I set myself up in a 'studio' in the recreation room. The *Surrealism of Science* and *Silence* (Pl. 16) were painted in the Erskine Avenue house. Both had a lot to do with the atmosphere of real silence: the baby was forever sleeping, so I couldn't play my jazz records loudly (no headphones then).

I had my second show at Isaacs in November/December '62 which included paintings like *Speak, Every Night* and *Prairie Landscape*. The exhibition was Pollocky (Jackson Pollock) and calligraphic, simple and very colourful, but it wasn't well received and only four or five paintings sold. In January '63 Allan Fleming, then art director at *Maclean's* magazine, gave me three editorial illustration jobs, which provided my only income that year except for the $4,000 from the Edmonton Airport Mural, most of which disappeared in bank loan repayments.

The year before, I had been chosen by a jury at the Federal Department of Transport to execute a mural at the International Airport in Edmonton, part of a Conservative Government plan for the new airports across Canada (Fig. 5). I had heard that Coughtry, Nakamura, Town and Gladstone were commissioned to execute works for Toronto International Airport and I was quite upset that I wasn't selected. Then I got the news from Ottawa that I'd been chosen to do the mural for the Quiet Lounge in Edmonton. It was to be on a curved surface, 7'8" x 27'. After meeting in Ottawa with the DOT committee and architects, I began to work on the studies and drawings for the maquette, but it wasn't until I received a cheque in December 1962 (the day Varyn was born) that I knew for sure my design had been accepted.

Jack Shadbolt already had installed his mural above the doorway at the Airport. I really liked his work – it is strong, 'Painters Eleveny' and cubistic, with the angular dynamics I like.

The mural I was to do was nothing but trouble from start to finish. In June '63 Heather, the baby and I headed for Alberta. The mural area was supposed to be ready July 1st, but when we got there we found it wouldn't be ready till August. The first night, after I'd set out my materials on the tables, $150 worth of paint was stolen. On the seventh day the painting was badly damaged; I repaired it and continued. On other occasions it was defaced – written and painted on – mostly, I assume, by labourers in the airport. Then, early in September, just when I felt I had completed my work and a man was coming from Ottawa to see it, someone defaced it again!

Heather and I were married in Edmonton. We flew back to Toronto in September and moved into the third floor of 842 Yonge Street. Things were very bad financially so Heather took a job in the CBC TV news department from October '63 to July '64. I babysat Varyn during those nine months, and it was while taking her out in the stroller every day, walking around Bay, Yonge and Bloor, that I came to know intimately all the shops displaying ladies' panties, undergarments, girdles, stockings and black winter boots. I nailed the canvas for *Bay-Yonge-Bloor* (Pl. 17) to the studio living-room wall and worked on it for twelve months. The next paintings I did moved away from abstraction: *Mountain Film, Metamorphosis,* and *I Remember Plastic Man*.

In September of '63 I began to teach part-time at the north branch of the YM and YWHA (the Hebrew Y) on Bathurst Street above Wilson Avenue. A vacancy had occurred when Gershon Iskowitz left and Bob Hedrick suggested I apply. They gave me several drawing classes and I enjoyed teaching

36 Locomotion 1972-73
  Acrylic and oil glazes on canvas
  72 x 80 in.
  The Isaacs Gallery, Toronto

40 Suspicion 1975
  Acrylic and collage on canvas
  60 x 72 in.
  The Isaacs Gallery, Toronto

those middle-class, middle-aged ladies. But in order to teach, I had to return to all that art school theory, so I started studying the Old Masters again and spent hours in the YMHA library copying information, particularly from the Italian Renaissance through to 1820 – art history I had never learned (OCA classes had ended in fourth year with Dutch and Flemish masters). Caravaggio, Velásquez and Zurbarán hit me the hardest, along with Vermeer who was denigrated at OCA when I was there 1952-56. Technique and method I had from Fred Hagan, and with my design and colour notes from OCA I had no trouble planning my courses. Those library days, though, were poignant and moving. I changed. I took teaching very seriously and, adapting to the intellectuality of that Hebrew environment, I re-educated myself. I did the teaching well, and it blossomed into art film classes and visiting the galleries' classes which I enjoyed immensely.

After six months, I was going out twice a week teaching all day and evenings at the YMHA. I was then asked to teach July and August at Manitou-Wabing Camp of Fine Arts near Parry

Sound. Heather and Varyn came with me; we ate well, we got healthy again. In the fall of '64 I was back at the YMHA and was also hired by Budd Feheley to work part time at Taber, Dulmage and Feheley Advertising. Dave McKay, my former boss at CBC, was once again my mentor.

Barrie Hale heard some of my lectures at the Y and also my lecture at the Art Gallery of Ontario in conjunction with the Post-Painterly Abstraction show there, organized by Clement Greenberg. Barrie felt that what I said about Post-Painterly Abstraction was so true, so witty, so perceptive that he wrote a whole column on me in *The Telegram.* I couldn't believe it, I didn't expect reviews of my teaching! For the next two years he exposed my attitudes to all, writing the best articles ever published on me and my work, and also on the artists at Isaacs and the rest of the Toronto scene. Barrie had come 'out of nowhere' and became our most important writer on art. His journalism was straight from the hip, straight from the shoulder, straight from the heart.

I began to draw again earnestly. Then it came to me as an illumination, as a thunderbolt! All the Old Masters had treated

Fig. 5 Mural 1963
       Oil and collage
       81 x 284 in.
       Edmonton International
       Airport

the female in a similar fashion: totally nude, devoid of pubic hair, or with a diaphanous covering over the pubic region. I thought, 'Why not do the same kind of picture with the same subject matter, yet clothe the women in modern underwear?'

In 1960 Gord Rayner had bought some really explicit 'skin books' in New York. The women posing wore real everyday undies. The photos were shot in bright artificial lighting and everything showed — moles, blemishes, everything! These New York-bought skin books showed a 'reality' I'd never seen before, anywhere. Looking at them was like looking through a keyhole: when you zoom in on something, even a human face and watch the lips move, it becomes erotic, because your focus is directed to such a small area.

The first work to deal with this new subject matter was called *The Dairy Queen Lover.* Then came *Psychic Virgin,* a pure white oil. *Dairy Queen Lover* was a bit more explicit. Then the 'break-through' ones, small black and white canvases of hips and thighs and stocking tops and garter straps, flat Greenbergian abstractions based on skin book photos. I made them as abstract as possible, yet simultaneously recognizable. The next step was another version of *Psychic Virgin* to which I added colour and colour shapes. It almost reached what I wanted to say, but not quite.

TDF 'let me go' at the end of January 1965 and then I was able to devote my full time to producing works in quantity and quality. I had done several by now, and began to swing with the whole idea and saw its possibilities. I can remember

Heather leaving in March. At that point I had hung *Psychic Virgin* in our hallway and had completed all the small, flat, simply coloured canvases like *Red Hot Mama, Red Garter* and *White Garter.* For these, I drew from the photographs in pencil, then painted in the colour, keeping the surface quite textureless. Drawing was the key, but I wanted to work with various points of view — technique, method and application of paint. One of those paintings, *Proposition 16,* was very tactile. It also had basic complementary colour contrasts. Then I thought, 'Why not have black-stained imagery, and use the raw canvas as a colour area?' *Gate View Girl* was one of the very first garterbelt paintings using black oil on the raw Belgian linen, a gold ochre colour (Pl. 20). I liked the way in which the oil stained into the canvas. At this point I wasn't thinking of staining as a mainstream post-painterly technique as Helen Frankenthaler had used it. I made other smaller pictures like *Crawl Girl, Answering Surface, Leap Girl* and *Fat Girl.*

The last work done before my show at Isaacs in April 1965 was the large canvas *Mother, Earth, Love* (Pl. 21). In it, I approached the figure from a landscape point of view, seen from above. I focused on the breasts, accentuating their size and shape by adapting the design of a French nursing brassiere. Then I suggested the panty-briefs and the garterbelt straps. At the same time, since I've always been deeply interested in astronomy, I made the breast areas suggestive of circular planetary orbits. This, then, was not only a landscape of earth viewed aerially, but a landscape of 'Mother Universe'.

Erotic Art and Collages (1965-1970)

Mother, Earth, Love was the last work before the Garterbelt Show opened (Pl. 21). *Room-Mates No. 3* was done just before *Mother, Earth, Love* and was a culmination of all the other work in that show (Pl. 18). What I really wanted to do in it, more than anything, was to keep the flatness. You'll notice in *Room-Mates No. 3* that one of the arms is missing; this was the first time I'd made a decision to leave out part of the anatomy. There are two females in the painting, the one in green less obvious than the one in red, and I was fearful that the police would bust Av or myself on some legality to do with depicting lesbianism. It was Kay Kritzwiser who coined the phrase 'Garterbeltmania'. I got very good reviews, and it has been the only show to date which sold well.

About a week before the show went up, I invited Barrie Hale to come over and see what I was doing, and he really liked my work. It was the first time since those write-ups he did about my '64 lectures that he had shown much interest. It was great to get that sort of affirmation from him. I believe the only other person I showed my paintings to was Arnold Rockman, who also liked them very much. He said 'they pulled together my draughtsmanship, colour sense and subject matter, which had up to that time been generally repressed' in *Canadian Art* (September 1965). Those earlier works of mine like *Burlesque Case* (Pl. 8) and *Smokeshop Sex Marauder* (Pl. 9) didn't show the subject so obviously.

Though my erotic drawings of women in underwear began as early as 1957, I did not focus on them until '64. I remember showing a portfolio of these to Budd Feheley, and it was partly on account of my drawing ability that he hired me to work at TDF. It was he who suggested a show of them to Av Isaacs. Most of the show in '65 at Isaacs was based on photographs. The drawings, though, were done from live models. I was convinced that they were too personal, but that is what art is all about. It was at my show at Av's in April '65 that Dorothy Cameron saw my work and liked it, and consequently decided to have a show of erotic art by her gallery artists. She had her show in May and that's history now – how the show got busted. My show was a month before but it wasn't busted. I hadn't depicted anything particularly obscene or pornographic; I had just depicted the female in underwear which at that time I suppose was a way to shock the middle class. But underwear was not just for its own sake; it was a matter of getting an obsession and a 'hang-up' out of my system.

Heather had left me in March but came back with Varyn in June, and the three of us went up to Manitou-Wabing Camp of Fine Arts where I was to teach for the second summer. After the first two weeks, as our attempt at reconciliation wasn't working out, I sent my wife and daughter home and stayed there alone to teach for the rest of July and August. They asked me to stay for the music camp after, which I did, and had a great time with all the musicians, teaching and playing. When I got back to Toronto, I found a place on Church Street where I've lived ever since.

It was then that I did the print for 'Toronto 20'. For that, I had my ex-wife Heather sit in a pail of orange acrylic paint, with her panties on, and then sit on blue railroad board that was bent over a barrel. I had discovered at Manitou-Wabing that if any moisture at all got on this particular board, it bleached the colour out of the cardboard. I don't think the technique has been used before or since; I was pleased with the effect it made. We did 121 or so and 100 went into the 'Toronto 20' print portfolio show in October at Jerrold Morris and Emilio Del Junco's gallery.

The same month, October 1965, the New School of Art started. There were only four people teaching that first year. I taught Renaissance drawing, drawing from the figure, and some 'Haganisms' that I'd learned from Fred at OCA plus what I had been teaching at the YMHA. Bob Hedrick was teaching along Bauhaus lines, with Itten-Albers colour theory and three-dimensional design. My assistant, Ken Lynwood, came in for the two and a half days a week I wasn't there, and Rosemary Kilbourne was to help Hedrick.

On October 19th, just outside the school on Markham Street, I noticed a terrific-looking girl, who turned out to be the model for my class that morning. Her body just knocked me out – it was exactly the *Mother, Earth, Love* body! Within a month Diane moved into the studio with me.

At that point I was drawing a lot, continuing the garterbelt theme. I did a lot of drawings of Heather of course, prior to our break-up in March 1965. Then followed a three-month period when I had between twenty-five and thirty models who came and posed in underclothes. The process of those drawings was really incredible because it was a matter of sublimating every sexual urge in order to use that energy to do the drawings. Some of those drawings would take up to four hours of concentrated, conscious staring at the girl's genitals. The first painting I did in the new studio was *White Trash*. This work developed from display items I'd found in a garbage can near Av's gallery, showing various kinds of stitches you could make with a sewing machine. I was working on that painting when Diane Pugen first came into my life.

Now I not only had a model, but I was also head-over-heels in love with her. Out of that came *Venus Evoked* (Pl. 22). We tried all kinds of posing positions that were unusual, so I could get newer vistas on the whole subject like the drawing looking up underneath that was on the cover of *Causeway* magazine, 1966. I did a lot of drawings of Diane, including *Venus Observed* and *Dogbone Girl*. Just about every other painting after that, up to the Tantric things, was based on Diane. She posed for *Girl* (Pl. 23), *Egypt Asleep* (Pl 24), *Leda and the Swan* and others up to *Listening to the Stones* (Pl. 26). In *Mothers and Daughters* (Pl. 25), although the basis for the imagery of the 1933 woman came from an old Simpson's catalogue, Diane posed for the figure. The 1966 girl was based on a photograph. Diane didn't exactly pose for *Yonique Metaphor – Prismadame* (Pl. 28), but she did pose for *Niagara Rainbow Honeymoon No. 1* (Pl. 29) and certainly for many hundreds of drawings. After I met Diane, my work was in a better state than it had ever been: I was really using my draughtsmanship and it seemed like everything was starting to make sense.

I stayed with the garterbelt subject matter through '66 and '67 and it culminated with the final painting of the series, *The Three Graces After Rubens* (Pl. 27). When I first started with the garterbelt idea, I wanted to do it in flat Greenbergian, simple colour, with line as the edge of colour area; no form, no volume, no illusion of space, very little texture. In *Gate View Girl* (Pl. 20), *Egypt Asleep* (Pl. 24), and *Leda and the Swan,* the flatness and the concern for design and line are the major characteristics. I seemed to go through the history of art: I started with medieval art in the first flat things, progressing to the most spatial, most three-dimensional, most painterly piece which was the Rubens copy, deliberately refuting the Greenberg reductivism (for the Rubens, see Fig. 6).

It was really a conscious progression, especially after *Venus Evoked* (Pl. 22) and *Venus Observed*. I wanted the subject matter to be more representational, and I can remember the sense of challenge I had prior to *Listening to the Stones* and during the two months I worked on it (Pl. 26).

Egypt Asleep was completed in two weeks, from the drawings to the finished work (Pl.24). Diane posed in its early stages: stylized alterations to representational drawings led to the final abstraction. I placed the Egyptian 'Ankh' (the sign of life) on the central area of white panties. The rings around each leg are based on Egyptian design and colour, each leg symbolizing a column as the entrance to a temple (these end with the inner contours of the feet). The breasts were abstracted into half circles for symmetry. While drawing the pose I noticed that, with the legs spread in such an extreme way, the tension on the garterbelt straps forced the central over-the-belly section of the waistband upwards; this created an equilateral triangle and became the basis for the inclusion of the pyramid. That observation became the 'hook' or symbolic means by which the work could continue to develop with definite Egyptian associations. Drawings from the middle to the end of December 1965 began with copies of Egyptian statuary. But, of course, the central idea is connected to *Psychic Virgin* paintings from late 1964 and the format of Tantric yonique metaphors from 1968. Drawings for close-in views also predate *Intimately Close-In* (1958; Pl. 4). The title for *Egypt Asleep* came from the pose of a sleeping woman in a supine birth-giving position, legs stirruped. When it was painted, Egypt under Nasser appeared to be unusually silent, as if asleep. The Six-Day War with Israel occurred in June '67.

Listening to the Stones portrays a woman who is in either a state of ecstasy or a state of meditation (Pl. 26). She is rapt, listening to the sounds of a turtle digging at the stones and pebbles in an aquarium. It is also possible that she is listening to the Rolling Stones' album 'Their Satanic Majesties Request'. The tune is probably 'She's a Rainbow'. The figure of the girl is depicted from a monocular (one-eyed) perspective viewpoint which accounts for the extreme foreshortening of the legs and torso, and the exaggerated size of the foot. Her foot is inordinately large because it is the part closest to the viewer. The large black brush which comes up and touches her knee is actually two feet closer to the viewer than her knee; I used that device to make a measure of spatial depth, and yet cancel the illusion. From the sole of the high-heeled shoe, up the figure to the face and top of the head would be, in proper ideal figure proportion, $8\frac{1}{2}$ heads (head unit = $7\frac{1}{2}$ ins.). So the woman is 5ft. 3ins. tall. Add the foreground space and the space behind her head, and there is a spatial depth of over 6

Fig. 6 Peter Paul Rubens
The Three Graces c. 1638-40
The Prado

feet. The paint brushes set up a foreground foil or vertical plane. On the wall, the garterbelt subject painting of a woman in panties, legs spread, provides the information about the genital area which is obscured in the painting of the listening woman.

For help with this painting, I looked again at the U.S. Famous Artists Course illustrators. I looked at Haddon Sundblom (who painted Coca-Cola ads in oil), at Robert Fawcett, at Norman Rockwell, at Ben Stahl, at dozens of old *Life* and *Collier's* and *Saturday Evening Post* magazines. Manet was no help, nor Ingres. Then I 'discovered' Bouguereau, Corot and Courbet. Doing *Listening to the Stones* was like going back to school but setting my own assignments. I found the photographic references I had for the figure's pose were not providing enough information; I had Diane pose so that I could solve the volume, form, light-and-shade problems. I stayed up all night after Di went to bed, painting the high-heeled red shoe as I would a still-life object, strung up by elaborate rigging at eye-level. *Listening to the Stones* was painted about Diane Pugen – of her and for her. When it was finished, I realized I had set for myself the painting problems I had encountered, not really to prove anything to myself but to prove that I could paint anything to her.

The next major task I set myself was to copy a representational painting by an artist I admired, and who had similar erotic interests – Rubens. *The Three Graces After Rubens* (Pl. 27) is really tongue-in-cheek, like Ward Kimball's *Art After-pieces* which alter famous paintings by known Masters in a significant way. The original Rubens, a little larger than my 5 x 5 ft. version, was painted 1638-40. It is one of his three paintings of The Three Graces. Rubens' treatment of the subject differs considerably from Botticelli's or Raphael's. It is thought out in terms of colour and surface luminosities, and abounds in intersecting diagonals and illusionistic devices which create spatial depth. Rubens accepted the nude woman as an organic fact, and his nudes are healthy and chaste.

In Rubens' painting the dancing figures, arms interlocked, are outside with trees to left and right. There is a bower of roses in the top centre where the two tree branches interlock like the Graces' arms. I did not like the grotesque drapery folds on the left, which resemble an ugly face, so I left them out of my version. Instead of trees I made a Roman arch, and placed the Graces inside in a bedroom alcove. On the right of the original there's a cornucopia out of which fruit tumbles. I abstracted this into a flat architectural ornament, and also changed the meadow to broadloom.

The bed was painted using our bed as a model. I had become very interested in painting drapery folds or creases, after I did *Jezebel* in '66. Studying Caravaggio, I discovered that his treatment of drapery folds was overly erotic; they resemble folds in human flesh, particularly the vaginal fold. Looking at figure painting from the Renaissance through nineteenth century, I found that drapery folds were used symbolically to represent genitalia (the artists had avoided delineating genitalia, even to the elimination of pubic hair). Upon that discovery my thesis became the bedclothes. Having painted the figure as exactly as I could from forty reproductions of the Rubens, I added brassieres, panties, garterbelts and nylons to the figures. It was necessary for Di to pose in these trappings to 'fit' them realistically on the Rubens nudes. I 'threw in' the green shoe on the right, and the red-striped (1967-style) 'op' panties, and instead of the rose bower I painted a stocking thrown over the arch. Then I put in a shadow of myself, nude, on the left where in the original, Rubens or some male figure is standing watching the Graces do their two-step.

It took four months of steady painting using Diane and the forty photographs. I always knew I could draw like Da Vinci, Michelangelo, Raphael, but I couldn't paint like them and it had always been an obsession with me to learn how. What I had never been taught at art school about anatomy, structure, lighting, the blending and modelling of flesh colours, was finally learned by doing that Rubens copy.

Yonique Metaphor – Prismadame is a close-in view of a woman with legs up, wearing nylons with seams and dark stocking tops, pulled on tightly without garterbelt (Pl. 28). The central area is a prismatic metaphor for the female genitals; the colour was based upon the colours of the spectrum, visible after a prism splits white light into rainbow hues. Drawings for the work were executed in New Jersey at the end of June 1967. The almost symmetrical grain of a wooden closet door suggested the subject. Drawings more obviously developed the wood grain pattern into contours of a model in the legs-up position. The Niagara Rainbow Honeymoon series began in April/May 1967 after a visit Diane and I took to Niagara Falls. In June at Fairleigh Dickinson University for a seminar, the first painting was about Niagara Falls, and then came Prismadame. The simile or metaphor for the female genitalia in that wood grain door led to the metaphors of the Butterfly, Orchid, Ladybug, Maple Sugar, and My Funny Valentine.

In Niagara Rainbow Honeymoon No. 1 the bed in the bedroom is the Niagara river and falls (Pl. 29). It represents the inescapable sound of the falls audible anywhere in the town. Also the bed as the falls represents rushing emotional and sexual anxiety. The woman is either dressing or undressing in a motel or hotel room. Is she a bride, the bride of Duchamp's Large Glass? Perhaps she is your mother? Your sister? Your aunt? Yourself? Maybe she is a hooker. Her facial expression is one of surprise mixed with expectancy, of innocence yet experience. The viewer has come upon her in the instant an action – a ritual to her – is in progress. Behind her, the spectrum of rainbow colours makes a frame as if she were before a mirror. The pose came from a skin-book photograph which, however, did not provide sufficient information to draw and paint the figure. In the original, the face and head were away from the viewer, in profile.

In Niagara Rainbow Honeymoon No 4 – AUM – The Sound of the Falls, the colourful symbol painted in rainbow colours is Aum, the first 'seed syllable' of the Tantric Yoga mantra 'Aum Mani Padme Hūm' (Pl. 30). This mantra is the most ancient and potent of prayers, because the words and sounds uttered aloud or chanted in the 'sound-mind' possess the most concentrated energy in the Universe. Om has three sound values A-U-M, and is the expression of the highest faculty of consciousness: 'A' is the waking consciousness, 'U' is the dream consciousness, and 'M' is the consciousness during deep sleep. The three come together as AUM. It is represented in the single word, symbolized in the painting, using stylized Tibetan Sanskrit (based on a gouache painting from Rajasthan, India, from the eighteenth century). This word-symbol for AUM represents one of the five wisdoms: the path to universality and freedom. AUM as a whole represents the all-encompassing cosmic consciousness on the fourth plane, beyond mere sounds, words or concepts. It is the consciousness of the fourth dimension! It is given the quality of a sound which the Vedics and Masters of Tibetan Mysticism associate with THE PRIMORDIAL SOUND. In my painting that 'primordial sound' is the deafening noise of Niagara Falls. In all my experience, no other sound equals the pitch, duration or volume of the Niagara river plunging through space. The drop of 176 feet is not extreme; the 2200 ft. width of the gorge and the volume of water falling make the din, the Ominous 'primordial' sound. It is said that one who is an expert at meditation can hear this sound through concentrated listening to the mind itself. AUM has been likened (in its three-fold one-ness) as equal to the Christian Trinity, God as Father, Son and Holy Ghost.

The subject is also in the Western European tradition of The Annunciation. From below, the viewer is looking through the legs of a woman – the backs of her legs and her torso are depicted. Let us suppose that only seconds ago, she removed the garterbelt which held up the stockings on her thighs. Suddenly facing her, there appears a blinding apparition in the form of the AUM symbol, eliciting from her a gasp of disbelief. Her entire self vibrates with cosmic recognition. To her has appeared the Spirit of God, the Holy Ghost, bringing 'the Word' to this woman, a virgin named Mary.

In the words 'and cast in her mind what manner of salutation this should be', I found the mystery that every painter from Leonardo to Burne-Jones visualized, the chance to depict the unknown. At the time, for me the problem was to unite the garterbelt imagery with that of Eastern (Tantric) art. In 1962 and 1970, when I received the news of fatherhood, I felt an AUM-like, thunderstruck, cosmic recognition of truth. After I thought about it I had an inkling of what Mary must have felt when she got her news.

Now connect the image of the woman in *Niagara Rainbow Honeymoon No. 1* with that in *No. 4* and, as if in a film, two different aspects of the same event are depicted. This 'Annunciation' is depicted in *Prismadame,* and also in *Egypt Asleep, Silence, False-True, Up-Tight News* and in other works of mine.

Many of the garterbelt subjects were based on magazine still-photos. They suggested ideas which could be developed, and led to posing a female model in such a way as to provide the obscured anatomical or lingerie information in detail. Photographs I had collected from 1950 to '67 (before *Penthouse*) were often insufficient because of poor lighting of the figure. I had discovered that black and white photographs of skin-book posed female models were more erotic than colour photographs. When I painted *Niagara Rainbow Honeymoon Nos. 1* and *4* and *Rosedale Rebellion '67,* my intention was to communicate a perceptual preference for figures painted in a neutral monochromatic grey-scale tonal range (Pls. 29-31). It was intended that the viewer associate the figures with black and white photograph images, which every male has seen, and which are a part of male voyeuristic experience.

I had a tough time after doing the Rubens copy and did a lot of commercial jobs, so I didn't have much time to paint. Arnold Rockman got me a job illustrating a music textbook for Gage and Company, using collage illustrations taken from the history of art. I did 161 collages and these gave me the idea of doing collages for my next show at Isaacs. Between '68 and '70, I made 31 more collages, like *Greece and Egypt* (Pl. 32), which were shown in September 1970. What really motivated them was an attempt to clean up the studio: I'd been saving the material for the collages for fifteen years!

Ever since art school I'd been plagued by my mind wandering while I was painting. Not when I was drawing the garterbelt things from models, but when I was painting *Niagara Rainbow Honeymoon No. 5* using a photograph as reference and Diane posing, all sorts of thoughts and ideas kept going through my head that had nothing to do with the work. So I bought a black notebook and put it on a desk near my canvas. Then, if something came into my head while I was painting, I'd write it down. I could get it out of my system this way, and be able to concentrate on painting. This writing down of everything that came into my mind, and collecting material from magazines and newspapers, became an obsession. As a result, by 1972/73 I was spending more time on the notebooks than I was painting. A lot of the ideas in the notebooks came out in collages.

When I was chosen as painting department chairman at OCA, it was out of sixty-four other candidates competing for that job, including artists from Europe, Great Britain, and the United States. During the summer of '70, while working on the collages, I had to prepare the teachers and the classes and the schedule for OCA. We had a real challenge to produce some new, young, good painters, for OCA had produced nobody really significant since Markle and Gorman. In that whole period between, say, 1956 and 1970 only a couple of names are important: painters David Bolduc and Greg Curnoe. And Curnoe has said that going to shows at The Isaacs Gallery really motivated him more than OCA itself.

Calligraphy (1970-1971)

After the collage show, I thought I should start working on some new paintings. I knew what was going on in the New York and European scenes with conceptual art, and articles such as Robert Morris's about the closure of painting with Stella in 1967. I started reading Greenberg about the importance of flatness, simplicity, and clean hard-edged imagery. Then it all came together. Clearing out my desk, I found brush pointings from as early as 1959, pieces of paper where I had pointed my water colour brush when I dipped it into the ink. Instead of wiping your brush on the rim of the india ink bottle, I'd learned from a Chinese fellow at the CBC to wipe the brush on a piece of paper and twirl it between your thumb and index finger. You would then make a stroke which pointed the brush, like Chinese calligraphy.

In late fall '70, I looked at all these pointings and thought, 'Why not blow these up in scale?' The current American rage was to enlarge some little diddle into a full-scale painting, move away from colour completely, using black shapes with lines around them for edges, against a field of raw cotton.

To begin, I would cut a little mat out of white paper with an opening of perhaps 1 1/2 x 3 or 2 x 2 inches, in proportion to the shape of canvas I was to do the painting on. I would drop this mat (in honour of Duchamp's three standard stoppages) a distance of one foot, so that it would fall randomly onto a sheet of brush pointings. Wherever the mat happened to fall, I would tape it down. That committed me: whatever was in that mat area would be the painting.

I had tried to copy freehand one of the small brush pointings onto a larger canvas but was unsuccessful; I couldn't achieve the exactness I wanted. Looking at these from a Duchampian 'ready-made' point of view, and from that of probability and from a surrealist point of view, there must be subject matter inherent in these marks made by a human being (myself). It was very necessary that they be transferred to the large canvases in exact scale, so that I lost none of the freshness or life. To achieve the accuracy I wanted, I would draw a grid on the original brush pointing, making, say, 1/8 inch squares. I would make a similar grid on the canvas in proportionately larger scale. Now, when I first started I thought the only way was to draw the grid in pencil, but then realized it could not be erased on the raw cotton duck. I finally seized on the idea of using thread (heavy duty black) to make the grid lines. (Chuck Close, the American portrait painter, and Roy Lichtenstein also use grid systems.)

Working on raw cotton duck and with a little water tension breaker in the acrylic paint, there was a chance that the paint would run down the canvas if I used an easel. So, true to the Frankenthaler, Noland, Louis and Jenkins way of working, I worked on all these paintings on a horizontal surface.

The painting of the canvases was very much a mechanical, boring business. First I would fill in along the edges of the calligraphy every stroke, every nuance, and then I would fill in the rest of the areas with black acrylic. Sometimes the black was mixed with Bocour blue or violet, ultra marine or dioxodine purple in order to get away from the browny colour of mars black, but I did want to preserve the integrity of black. The more I did, the more I allowed a little bit of staining and bleeding within the calligraphic shapes; so while they might have a black edge to them, there would be colour inside.

I was working here with a basic but important artistic idea: the balance or the imbalance, the symmetry or asymmetry of spatial areas. The raw cotton duck was to be infinite space, the black areas the image, the positive statement, the yin (male) part of the painting, the yang (female) being the cotton duck.

Seeaph and *Concorde* in this retrospective are two of the most successful (Pls. 33 & 34). *Seeaph* was the very first after I'd learned to use the thread. It was not painted on cotton duck but on a piece of Belgian or French canvas with a very heavy weave. By the way, paintings such as these were named using the sound of syllables from various words; *Seeaph,* for instance, really meant 'see Av' (Av Isaacs). *Concorde* I feel was one of the best images the mat-dropping created, because it is so dramatic. *Seeaph* and *Concorde* (like many paintings I've done) may be hung with any edge as bottom or top. *Concorde* was so named because it's painted with mars black and alizarin crimson, plus another dark reddish pigment producing the colour of Concord wine. The Modern Jazz Quartet made an album called Concorde, to do with the Place de la Concorde, and my title came out of these associations.

About thirty-one of these paintings were in the November '72 show at The Isaacs Gallery. I've had remarks by other artists since, that perhaps I hung too many, that I should have weeded out a few. But I was so profoundly moved by the whole idea of doing them, and over a period of two years, that I really wanted to hang all the best ones. I must have done at least 40 of them, some having more colour than others. After the show was up I sent reproductions of slides and black and white photographs to Robert Motherwell. (I'd met him in 1970 at OCA.) Generally speaking, the critics didn't say much. Kritzwiser related them to Franz Kline's black and white works and I think completely missed the point.

As with so many of my one-man exhibitions, nothing sold while the show was hanging. So I was very depressed and didn't paint for about six months; just kept teaching. I was exhausted after two hectic years: the year as director of OCA in '70, then being a director of the New School of Art in '71, having broken my ribs twice in 1970 (in April and again in June), and then working on all those black and white things. Partly it had to do with the fact that, at the same time that I was painting, I was really 'into' the occult, I-Ching, Seznec's book *Pagan Gods in the Renaissance,* Tibetan Sanskrit. I was into Tantra, still reading about it rather than looking at pictures. I was into magic, astrology, numerology, Pythagoras; *The Great Teachings of All Ages* by Manly Palmer Hall; Hermes Trismegistus; the Egyptian Greek and Roman gods, the Mayan and Inca gods. And I began to get a terrible feeling that these paintings were related to my readings! Some of the paintings in my studio were with me as 'presences'; I had a 'Muse' while I did them. Though they originated simply from brush pointings, ink (originally made from ivory) is now made from burned bones of animals. Out of all this study of the occult I got into a 'mind state'. I wouldn't call it meditation exactly, but it was almost the state of mind of a conjurer. I was 'conjuring', ready to cast a spell.

I had complete control of these paintings: my mind seldom wandered. I used to wear earphones while working so I wouldn't hear anybody. And I would have the complete input of the audio of jazz, classical, romantic or baroque music, while working on these very systematic calligraphic paintings.

Locomotion was the second painting I did in 1972, after completing and exhibiting the calligraphic series (Pl. 36). Barrie Hale once said to me, 'You've got to escape that obvious Robert Motherwell influence, Dennis.' I have, but I had to let the influence run its course. From 1960 until 1975, I turned to Robert Motherwell's *Elegy to the Spanish Republic* paintings, for stimulation, for courage and for motivation. It was heroic subject matter; he painted works dedicated to what (until recently) was a lost cause — Spain as a democracy. Motherwell has aptly said, 'The history of Modern Art tends at certain moments to become the history of modern freedom'.

Politics aside, what has so continually enchanted me, in Motherwell's paintings, are those heavy, yet floating, huge elliptical black shapes flanking a vertical bar. More than any of the other Abstract Expressionists, I like that look of gestural freedom in a Motherwell. In order to understand action painting, I found it necessary to put Kline, De Kooning, Rothko, Newman, Twarkov, Reinhardt, Francis, Rauschenberg and Hofmann all aside, and concentrate on one of their number. Who answered my questions — is the work painterly? strong? can derivations be made, yet be original? etc. Motherwell won, hands down (or hands up!).

From 1960 to 1965 I was learning from his work. After the calligraphy of 1970-72 when I got back to abstraction, the Motherwell pull was still there. This time I decided to let it all hang out. Influence? No less than six works between '72 and '76 exploited the influence, and in so doing I let the crutch burn itself out. Without it, there would have been no *Locomotion* (Pl. 36), no *Bad Good Friday* (Pl. 39) and no *Evidence* (1959). No profound motive for having returned to abstraction.

Locomotion, while influenced by Motherwell, has its origin in a black calligraphic work I did in 1971. On either side of *Locomotion* are two rectangles which show their farthest-away vertical edges, smaller in proportion to their edges along the right and left of the canvas. They are meant to guide the viewer into the illusionistic space suggested by the blue field. The major central image with its flanking calligraphy creates drama as in the *Concorde* painting. Movement is suggested. I wanted that same feeling in *Locomotion.* The two large calligraphic strokes on each side of the central image might be read as fenders, or as legs, almost as if some kind of huge insect or crustacean is moving across the field from left to right. *Locomotion* has to do with movement, though I didn't know there was a dance tune on the hit parade at that time with the same title. The Loco part of Locomotion means 'crazy'; the thing in *Locomotion* is moving crazily to the right. I achieved something here that I hadn't achieved very often. Beginning to shed the Motherwell influence, I hit on a really strong image, my own. The lower central dark shape didn't work without the extension above it; it was necessary to compose it asymmetrically that way. There still seemed to be something missing, so I clarified the drawing with orange pastel (the complementary colour to the particular blue I had used). The pastel is drawn very freely, those curved strokes done at arms' length. I often work this way on large canvases. *Locomotion* is one of my favourite paintings.

Up-Tight News was done in '73/74 (Pl. 38). During the period 1972-74 I became interested in Kasimir Malevich, El Lissitzky, the suprematists and constructivists. I read Malevich's book on art. His definitions of purity and suprematism, his use of colour and geometric shapes and his concern for space had a profound effect on a number of my works. *Up-Tight News* was one of them and an earlier one, *Neo-Suprematist Painting,* another. From these sources I became very involved with straight lines, rectangles and clear shapes, with pure colour made by several transparent glazes, and a new clarification of imagery. In a sense they relate back to the first two or three paintings from '58-60: *Intimately Close-In, Intimate* and *Burlesque Case* (Pls. 4, 7 & 8). These have a similar geometric feeling for spaces and large areas and shapes, but are more bio-morphic.

Up-Tight News is based on part of De Kooning's *Gotham News,* particularly the lower right-hand corner, where there is a very strong red and white. The knife and brush strokes in that part of the painting are dramatic gestures. I took this and abstracted it in flat suprematist terms. Gotham was a mythical, totally immoral city so this painting of mine alludes to Toronto as Canada's Gotham. Instead of calling it 'Gotham News' it's 'Up-Tight (City) News'. It's a very tight painting done with acrylic and masking tape, with De Kooning shapes abstracted and made flatter, more suprematist. There is no real concern with spatial depth; the colours help to flatten it, and are more intense than in any other work of mine. I used colour definitely for colour's sake. There is hue contrast, complementary contrast, and simultaneous contrast areas, vibration

edges and successive contrast. *Up-Tight News* summed up all my colour background to 1974. The canvas has a white margin around it; it seemed logical that the central image be isolated on this white, nearly square field.

Across the top of the painting, like a title, are alphabet letters, as if the painting were a cover for a magazine called *Up-Tight News*. At that time Nixon was President, and there was trouble in our own federal government. And the most common expression you heard anywhere was 'up tight'. The painting also came out of the influence of my daughter Maihyet, who by '73/74 was doing a lot of printing of letters she made up, and drawing alphabets of her own trying to print and write English.

Suspicion was done in 1975 and concerns a strange and very disturbing emotion (Pl. 40). It was a difficult painting to do. I wanted to make a simple statement, developed from the large abstract shapes of Motherwell and others who are not strictly geometric abstractionists. The two large dark shapes are like sails, though they could also be the bottoms of two large calligraphic strokes. With these, there's a definite circular motion from centre top to the middle of the canvas. The other elements are either fragments about to reassemble, or else they are being broken asunder from some original whole, in the sense of disintegration. The painting is like *Locomotion*: freezing in time and space a particular action that seems to be at quite a distance. All the peripheral vision activity is limited to simple colour and shape, so that the main image not only gives a strong effect of manganese blue on a white field but there is power in these two similar forms, one large and one smaller and apparently farther away. The closer, larger shapes exaggerate and increase the scale of the actual event about which I was suspicious. Ambiguously, it can be read in the reverse spatial order: the vertical shape on the left and the larger crescent shape may be the real event, and the upper right corner a shadow or reflection, the suspicion of the real event. When I was working on the canvas, this use of a repeat, of a smaller echo, a shadow or reflection in the upper corner seemed to make the painting work. The two dark shapes are not exactly the same, just as an event can happen which has a particular configuration to it, and that event, when one is suspicious about it, will take on an entirely different curvature or shape. The suspicion is clearly not the reality.

This painting has a lot of energy in it, psychic and sexual. Worry, concern, fear, all these emotions are in the painting and have to do personally with me. *Suspicion* has to do with that mind-bending kind of self-torture when, after weighing particular acts and types of behaviour, you have something to be suspicious about yet you have no factual evidence to support it. When I was working on it, I was going through a terrible state of mind, thinking that my wife was unfaithful.

Bad Good Friday is exactly what the title implies, a painting completed on Good Friday (Pl. 39). I get very depressed in March because it takes so long for spring to get here. However, February through April is a very interesting time of year, when everything is in a changing state – winter and action and snow and thaw. *Bad Good Friday* was done in that kind of period. *Bad Good Friday* emerged directly from seeing 'Ben Hur' and 'The Robe' on television.

With those Motherwell elliptical shapes *Bad Good Friday* also has a lot to do with the imagery in Motherwell's Spanish Elegy series, usually the genitals of a bull which are cut off, along with the ears and tail, after the bull has been killed in a bullfight. *Bad Good Friday, Father Dead, Mother Well* and *Locomotion* all refer to male genitalia. *Bad Good Friday* was a result of being sexually exhausted. What was it Gertrude Stein said? 'You must empty yourself completely before you empty yourself on the canvas'.

There are also Christian references in the painting. The bowl is supposed to represent the bowl of medication Christ was offered before He was crucified. Also it stands for the bowl from which the vinegar-soaked sponge was taken to dab the spear cut in His side. There's a reflection or shadow or echo of a cross in that painting. It's really an abstract statement about the crucifixion.

Whereas Easter's meaning is the resurrection and the light, I get very depressed at that time of year. I'm generally suspicious and at that time especially so because of the Ides of March. That's when I did the painting. It's a painting about death and depression, dark blue midnight, cold winter March sky, huge swollen gonads, splatters of blood, and everything from Christianity's story, the cross and all such imagery. Many abstractionists shy away from theological themes but a lot of my work has to do with religious convictions, whether Oriental, Indian, Hindu, Buddhist, Jewish or Christian. Painting, I feel, is a religious activity.

Coming Down was done as the last work for my show at The Isaacs Gallery in February of '76 (Pl. 42). Coming down means coming down from drugs, coming down means emotionally, coming down after sex, coming down after eating, coming down the stairs, coming down from heaven. Coming down, going down, falling down. And it has to do with the way the paint is coming down the canvas.

The entire work was done with a piece of 2 x 4 and small bits of wood. The middle image was created by putting pools of acrylic paint along the wide side of the 2 x 4. Then I picked up the 2 x 4 (with allusions to Christ and the Cross) and walked over to the canvas stapled on the wall. Then, carefully holding the 2 x 4 over my head with the paint on the top surface, I slapped it against the canvas so that all the paint would adhere and, in the slapping motion, spatter. Then I let the 2 x 4 slide down, alternating the pressure and lack of pressure on it, making vertical columns of paint on the canvas. Having completed that part I poured pools of acrylic onto a silk-screen squeegee to make the diagonal across the bottom. The area near the centre where there's a bit of white and some rather beautiful paint motion was done with small pieces of wood. I squeezed acrylic on to these and then pressed them against the canvas, letting the wood slide around. I had no idea what pattern or what colour would come out, what would mix or what wouldn't. So it's a mixed motion painting, the result of motion action, which is like action painting, and it was done with twentieth-century technique. The squeegee and the scraper and painting with wood have been around since the post abstract expressionist period of the late 1950s, and all those years I've been painting with brushes and drawing with pencil.

In *Strophic Slide* and in *Coming Down* I tried these newer things out for the first time on a large scale. I wanted works that came out the first time, without having to make repeats of them. Both were cases of 'beginner's luck'. They were extremely easy to do, though it is not the kind of facility I have with a brush or pen and pencil. They simply required very little physical effort.

Nastaliq Automatique is a large Islamic-like calligraphic area of red against a blue field (Pl. 43). The red has paint spatters and action painting activity, and sets up vibrations with the blue, a simultaneous contrast colour. Designing the large image was very difficult; it went through several stages on the canvas. I wanted a single stark figure on a ground using colour, with Islamic calligraphy as subject matter. I didn't take the painting deliberately from anything Islamic. It was only after I had completed it that I realized how much it resembled Arabic art. I could find nothing exact, but the feeling for Islamic art is there.

At that time, where could an artist have a show? He couldn't, there was no place. You had to exhibit through the societies that existed then like the Ontario Society of Artists, The Royal Canadian Academy, The Canadian Society of Painters in Water Colour, Canadian Society of Graphic Arts, etc., etc., etc. For those shows you had to submit work to be juried and you had to pay fees to enter the exhibition, you had to have your work matted and framed and everything and it used to cost a lot of money, but I was determined to get recognition and I made up my mind to enter every available society show, so over that period of 1957-60 approximately, I exhibited in just about every one of the possible shows. Fortunately, they accepted a lot of my work, but I did get a number of rejects. Several rejects which were returned to me by freight or express never got picked up by me at the CPR station because I couldn't afford the cost of the freight charges of the works coming back from shows. At least five of the things left there were sold at auction. I remember once I had a guy phone me up who said, 'I just bought a painting of yours for ten dollars,' and I said 'Where?' and he said, 'At a CPR auction, it's about 48 x 60 inches and it's oil and pretty thick and, boy, did I ever get a bargain.' But in order to eat and work you had to put up with anything.

I remember the Women's Committee of the Art Gallery of Ontario. Were they ever important! In 1960 I had three things in their show, in '62 two and in '63 five, and in '63 they invited all the Quebec artists such as Tousignant and Hurtubise to show at the AGO Then there was the Women's Auxiliary of the Vancouver Art Gallery who had a show every year too. There was the Young Contemporaries exhibition in London at the Public Library and Art Museum, the Hadassah shows in Toronto and the auctions at Eaton's and Simpson's.

At that point there were only three commercial galleries in Toronto: Av Isaacs' Greenwich Gallery was started in '56, then the Gallery of Contemporary Art opened in '57 and I was represented by them, along with Bob Hedrick, Kazuo Nakamura, Tom Hodgson and most of the guys from Painters Eleven, but it only lasted one year so all of us had to find another dealer. I went to the Park Gallery and had a show there in '58 after having a show at GCA in '57.

As for collectors and collections at that time: Imperial Oil and CIL were buying, so were Mrs. John David Eaton, Mrs. Zacks, Charles Band and the Bronfmans in Montreal, and that

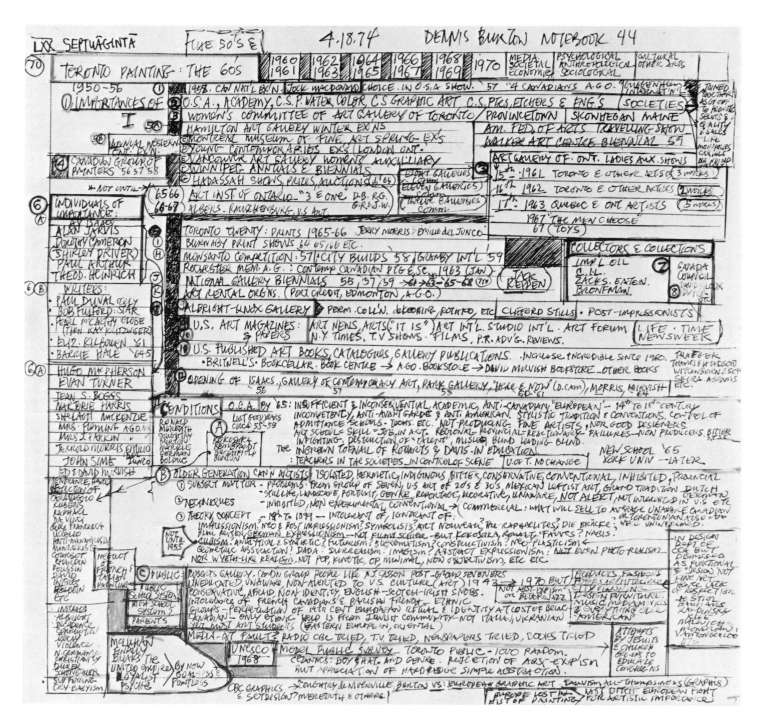

was about it. By 1961 none of us had been left out of most of those collections. It became the thing then for artists to go to those people's houses and drink their booze and talk about art until four or five o'clock in the morning. Those were the wonderful party years. We were all reading magazines to find out about the New York scene: *Art International* and *Art and Architecture* with articles and reviews by Doré Ashton, later on *Studio International* and *Art Forum;* and there were articles in *Life, Time,* and *Newsweek.* We used to buy *The New York Times* every Sunday and read the reviews by John Canaday of artists of New York, etc. There was the odd TV show about artists and some films, but the big thing was a lot of PR and advertising and reviews in all that American stuff, and so we thought, that's the way it should be in Toronto; but it was a hard thing to get rolling. It did eventually happen and I want to mention some really important people: Allan Jarvis, Dorothy Cameron, Paul Arthur from *Canadian Art* and especially Theodore Heinrich of the Royal Ontario Museum (who came to my studio in '61 because I had asked him to look at my work to give me a Canada Council recommendation). Paul Duval was an art writer and critic whom a lot of people put down, but what he wrote in *The Telegram* every week was good art criticism. He wrote about my work and often said nice things. Robert Fulford then started writing about art in *The Toronto Star,* Pearl McCarthy was in *The Globe and Mail* and she was really good, she said what she thought, she knew her stuff and it wasn't just art writing, it was solid criticism. I can remember the second one-man show I had, she put it down hard but, you know, it really meant something to me to have someone tell me what was wrong, because we were all running around like rats in a cage trying to find a way out, wondering what we were doing wrong, wanting somebody to help us, and she used to tell us where it was at. When Pearl died, Kay Kritzwiser took over at *The Globe and Mail;* then Elizabeth Kilbourn started to write in *The Star* instead of Fulford. She used to fill two columns, page length. I tried to save all of them, for they were really incredible, so emotional and full of beautiful adjectives. I remember how she raved about Mike Snow, but she was simply telling the truth to the Philistines. Then Barrie Hale came along about '64 and saved the scene because it had just started to 'go down' and he brought it back to life in *The Telegram*'s 'Showcase'. His boss, Tom Hedley, felt that it was very important to write about art and

artists — thank God! There was an article about the Group of Sex — Coughtry, Town, Markle, myself and three others who were supposed to be the 'Canadian Group of Seven of Erotic Art'.

There were other important people — for instance, Hugo McPherson, an art collector, art writer and former director of the National Film Board. If he wasn't at your show opening you felt you weren't worth anything. Another really important guy was Evan Turner, director of the Montreal Museum of Fine Arts. One day he said to me — I'll never forget it — 'You know, you and your friends, your work is so good, you have no reason to feel any kind of smallness or lack of identity compared to the Americans. They've got more of a network behind them of galleries, museums, publicity, write-ups, monographs, catalogues; they can afford it down there, and there's ten times more people. You guys should all leave this God-forsaken Canada and go to the States, because you're all good, there's no sense in staying here, it won't take you long to get a good dealer with the stuff you've already done and you'll make it down there.' Ronald had proved that by going down there and talking Sam Kootz into paying him a salary to paint abstract expressionism. He got his stuff into every important museum across the States and a lot of his work was as good as, or better than, the big men. Then there was Jean Boggs; when she took over at the AGO and then the National Gallery, things started to change.

I used to hang out at the corner of Bloor and Yonge, at Britnell's, the Pilot Tavern, and Isaacs — it was a triangle, and I'd be in Britnell's more than in the other two sometimes because that's the only place that had the most recent publication of art books and we were all dying to see the new colour Klines reproduced. About that time the publishing industry in the United States and England started to accelerate because all the Praeger paperbacks came out, then the Thames and Hudson paperbacks. The Wittenborn & Schulz books like Kandinksy's *Concerning the Spiritual in Art,* Jean Arp's *On My Way, The Dada Painters and Poets* by Robert Motherwell, Apollinaire's *The Cubist Painters* and Amédée Ozenfant's *The Foundations of Modern Art,* printed in 1952, were already in our libraries. *The Documents of Modern Art* from Wittenborn & Schulz, most of which are now unavailable, were the textbooks of modern painting before Sam Hunter's *Modern American Painting and Sculpture* which was first printed in 1959.

The group of artists known as Painters Eleven (1953-60) was of great importance. The first time I met Kazuo Nakamura was at a Painters Eleven show where I was introduced to him and said, 'How ya doing, Nak?' I remember him stepping back and saying 'How do you do?' — he's so quiet, so beautiful. The only other time I remember encountering him turned out to be a major event. It was on Bloor Street and, you know, when two artists meet each other on the street, they do stop and talk, because when you're out there in the environment it's just like hell, so I said 'Hi', and he said 'Hi', and I said 'You know, I've been looking at all the art magazines and I really don't like what's going on, and there's nothing there that interests me, and how do you feel about that?' and he had this book behind him all the time and he finally said 'Well, here', and he handed me a *Scientific American*. That was in 1960 and I have had a subscription to that magazine ever since. Nakamura turned me on to that; I've learned so much from *Scientific American* because of him. The day I got it, I couldn't understand the articles because the technology was so far out, but I enjoyed reading something new and I liked the diagrams. (I buy two copies every month so I can clip articles out for the New School students to read.) I've got every article they've ever done on physics and perception and psychology; I've learned more about the eye and how to teach drawing from what psychologists found out about perception than from any art texts. None of the minimalists in the States who were interested in 'reductivism' (getting rid of everything unnecessary in the painting) ever did anything quite so lyrical or simple as some *Scientific American* illustrations. Nakamura's still using the graph and science, and math and physics as imagery in his paintings; it's beautiful. Nak has been a very profound influence on a lot of artists in Toronto. They won't admit it because they don't realize it until they see his work again.

Harold Town was very important to me and to most of the other guys my age because he was an individual, a maverick, who had made it regardless of the societies and everything else. He set himself the task of doing abstract painting and doing it well, and a lot of people put him down because of his success, but it's like envying Rubens for having invented mass production. Town is terribly prolific. He knows what he's talking about — I love his writing more than his painting, and it's wonderful to hear him talk because he's just hilarious. I've

always seen Town as a kind of Glenn Gould in painting, he's an incredible draughtsman and has a lot of facility. I think he's the only artist in Canada, except for maybe Alex Colville, Jack Chambers, Ken Danby and a few of the 'new realists', who makes a living solely from the sale of his work.

What were the incentives and motivation? Why paint? What was the goal orientation? For me from 1955 on, it was the financial and media success of the American abstract expressionists, along with the subsequent celebration of their cultural achievement internationally, and that was what I identified with and so did everybody else I know. One of the things that painters felt around Toronto was, let's finally rout these funky jazz musicians and replace them as cultural heroes, and we all went on a pressure thing to replace the jazz musicians as the culture heroes just as they'd done in the States. I'm telling you, that was a major motivation! Now, where could you become a culture hero? It was at the new independent galleries, of course. At those openings that we used to have in the 50s and 60s we had jazz playing in the back rooms, there was always Scotch and other strong booze and the openings went on till midnight. There were marvellous parties afterwards at the artists' studios and people got to now each other: the coterie, the collectors, everybody was at those things, and then people began to play jazz at them, which led to the Artists' Jazz Band.

As early as 1952 we were into bebop, jazz, electronic music, John Cage, blues and rock, and I mean not just me but all the guys I know. We were into James Joyce, Dostoyevsky, Norman Mailer and Nat Hentoff, Samuel Beckett, William Burroughs, Sartre, Mallarmé, Rimbaud, Apollinaire, Breton, E.E. Cummings, Dylan Thomas, Ogden Nash, and especially Jack Kerouac, way back about '57. And films too, Antonioni, Von Stroheim, Eisenstein, Bergman, Fellini, the Polish and Czech films — we went to every one of those. We used to buy *Seven Arts* magazine, which had articles by Gian-Carlo Menotti, Pinter, Ionesco, Genet and McLuhan. Coughtry once did a poster for a play by Ionesco, *Rhinoceros*. Back about 1960 more and more people were getting into the grass thing and their sensibilities were changing and so were their perceptions. There was an incredible run of comedians and I remember Mort Sahl, Lenny Bruce, Sid Caesar, Lord Buckley and Carl Reiner. Later came Bill Cosby, Nichols and May, and Mel Brooks. We would go to each other's studios and watch those guys on television and fall down laughing because they were so far out. There were a couple of things we were reading which motivated us: a little book by Norman Mailer called *The White Negro,* and Seymour Krim's *Making It,* which is where that phrase came from.

My mind completely changed, I became what all the other guys became, but it wasn't due to drugs, it was a whole new sensibility, it was 'go out and get what you want'. Don't buy – sell! – which meant that we had to be kind of used car salesmen for our art. The important thing then was to be at every opening and anywhere there was action – to be there in person and come on strong – and it worked. Most of the kids I teach at the New School have no goal orientation, no motivation, no incentive, no drive – 'everything's phoney anyway, capitalism's a drag' – and it's really hard to teach them. We didn't know it would go like this, we really didn't know, we thought it would just keep on going like we were, energetic, heavy – but it all changed.

To recap, I'd say that conditions were bad at the outset, around 1957, and they haven't improved much at all, except in some personal cases. It's a little better for the young artists than it was for us, but it's not really changed, and I ask myself, Who's to blame? What are we going to do? Is education the answer? You know what Marsden Hartley (1870-1953) said in in 1921? 'Painting in America [Canada] is like a patent medicine or a vacuum cleaner. It can hope for no success until at least 90 million people know what it is.' Education is helping by creating an audience but you seldom sell your work to ex-students or because of an article in a national magazine, or from a television interview.

I'm interested in expressing myself through surface, as well as through colour, line, shape, form and all the other analytical technical words that describe what painting is.

As it's said in jazz – 'it don't mean a thing if it ain't got that swing' – it's not what you do, but how you do it. The period of the garterbelt paintings, 1964-68, was the only time I was ever concerned with subject matter in my work, because in the garterbelt paintings the girls and women in their underclothes concerned me more than technique. While I was involved with the subject of 'what' to paint, the more I understood how to present the female in underclothes; and the more confident I got about the subject matter in my own life and in my paintings, the more I became concerned with 'how' to do them. Thus there is a progession in the garterbelt paintings from flat abstraction, using only black and white, through to the full blown Baroque treatment of *The Three Graces After Rubens* (Pl. 27).

I think all the concern for 'how', and for surface, aside from subject matter, goes back to my training at the Ontario College of Art. When I painted from life I tried to make a direct painting using the Old Master traditional technique; that is, having a good drawing in line and having, with that drawing, a good tonal study of the subject matter in black, grey and white. Colour was incidental and added almost in a water colour way. In second, third and fourth year painting at OCA, there was more concern with a technical look and a technical way of painting that resembled impressionism. There were a few people in the class who were working out of other traditional methods, such as Fred Orchard who worked from the burnt umber raw umber darkness, with brush drawing moving towards the lighter colours and towards white and black as the final strokes to complete the work, very much in the tradition of the Dutch Masters. There were others who painted thinly first, not in glazes but in turpentine washes, moving through those washes toward texture, impasto, scumbling, and deeper texture.

My work from art school could be described as looking 'slick' because in painting the figure I didn't want texture, surface or facture to have much to do with the image, while at the time I was using a lot of damar varnish mixed with linseed oil and turpentine as my medium. Therefore, my work in third and fourth year was quite shiny and slippery looking, and this was long before the invention of matt fixatives. When I moved into abstraction in 1955/56, I also retained the glossy damar varnish look in my early work, but gradually eliminated it as a total look when I got more interested in facture, as a result of seeing works by De Kooning and Kline and the mattness of Rothko, Reinhardt and the other American abstractionists. I was always interested in the surface Graham Coughtry was getting in his work around '55/56 which was coming out of the impressionist technique (brush strokes made by the hogs-hair in the 'Monet water-lilies' type of facture). I didn't work in the impressionist style until my first one-man show at GCA in 1957

In the beginning, when I was in art school, all my paintings from life, my portraits, my still life paintings, generally had an all-over shiny surface. It was in still life paintings that I began to change technically, mostly as a result of the influence of Jock Macdonald who taught me when I was in my second and third years. His own paintings were very matt and dry-looking. I can remember that my still life paintings for him were semi-abstract and I wasn't a bit interested in creating the illusion of space. I didn't get away from using that damar varnish shiny look until around '56/57 when I was working on the paintings for a show at GCA. The use of MG white, an oil titanium white made by Grumbacher, which was very chalky and dry, pre-cipitated a change in the look of the paintings and I began to mix less varnish in the medium. After that Monet-like hogshair brush show of '57, I moved into abstract expressionist paint-ing, more concerned with facture and texture and large flat areas. I was working in my studio on Bedford Road, and I was doing abstractions like the one submitted to the Windmill Point competition, and to the Monsanto Painting competition, and also like the painting called *Abstraction No. 4* in the first or second Biennial at The National Gallery of Canada.

In those days of working at the Bedford Road studio, I gradually worked with less damar varnish. I discovered a cheap permanent white that I could mix with other colours and use as a ground. It was called CIL Oval Primer and I would buy the primer at a hardware store, pour off the excess oil and then use this precipitated white titanium primer as the white. In those days, I was working on masonite, which often I didn't prime but allowed the raw brown look of untempered maso-nite to show through some of the oil. Paintings like *Intimately Close-In* (Pl. 4), *Evidence, Cooks White Instead of Orange on a Tabletop Landscape* and most of the works between '57

and '60 were done on masonite using this CIL Oval, which dried quite matt and was very useful as a white for all pur-poses. I continued to use the MG white and other paint com-pany brands of oil white in my work, and when I wanted to build texture, I used the MG white in order to create the brush-stroke-look or the look of facture. Knowing, from the excellent technical background I got from Carl Schaefer, that latex and house paints were not permanent and not as good quality as artists' paint, I never used them. When I worked with enamel in '62/63 for my Isaacs Gallery one-man show, I used a very high quality sapolin enamel bought at a hardware store because I couldn't afford artists' oil paint. I used it for such paintings as *Speak, Everynight, On My Own,* and the works that Ed Mirvish bought from the show. I was very careful to use the enamel in proper technical ways, but again it was quite shiny and in order to cut down on its varnish content, I used it thinly, almost like water colour.

Very seldom have I worked with transparent colour, except in '57/60 when I did a lot of glazing. There was one thing about my paintings from that period that gave them a different look from my contemporaries' and that was glazing with damar varnish, along with the texture and facture in an abstract ex-pressionist style. No one else was glazing at that time; no one was using traditional oil technique. Generally, it seemed as if painting in oil had moved from impressionism and post-impressionism directly into abstract expressionist action painting, without any of the fine points of historical technique like glazing being retained. Since they interested me I tried to get impasto, scumbling, glazing and the full range of techni-cal possibilities into my oil paintings, and that is the distinctive thing about my paintings — the look of the surface.

Gord Rayner discovered things about acrylic long before anybody else, although I can remember Richard Gorman being the first painter on the Toronto scene to work with a-crylic. When we saw Rick's first acrylic paintings we were quite upset by their surface and by the look of acrylic. It seemed he couldn't control the acrylic in the same way he could control oil; none of us were able to at first. I was one of the last people to work with acrylic. I don't think I began to work with it until '65. *Mothers and Daughters* (Pl. 25) has some acrylic in it as well as oil, as does *Mother, Earth, Love* (Pl. 21). These were technical ventures on my part to find out what acrylic was like. I don't think I fully mastered or understood acrylic until after 1972. So it took me 7 years! I can remember Gord Rayner's early Magnetawan paintings. He would pour acrylic onto the painting – sometimes the puddle would be an inch thick. Then, in drying, it would crack. At first I was quite upset by the surfaces Rayner was getting with his poured acrylic, simply because they did crack, but then I began to realize that the cracking was intentional, that acrylic is a permanent substance and the cracking was not the kind of cracking that happens to an oil painting. Gord has always broken new ground technically, he innovates out of never having had to conform to art school do's and don'ts. Still, nobody paints a surface in oil or acrylic as I do.

I think I've been misunderstood when it comes to my abstractions, because I don't think it is realized that each abstraction is a single work, quite separate from others before or after it. Most of my abstractions are related to the city environment in terms of surface, facture and texture. When I worked in series, in the garterbelt period, the collages, and the calligraphic paintings, there was little concern for facture and texture. When I do abstractions, as from '55 to '65 and from about '69 to '76, I'm interested in each abstraction as a single work and not as part of a series. It has been said that 'to work in series is the chief defense against the risk of misinterpretation.' Each time I have worked in series my work is misinterpreted in the extreme! Therefore when people speak of a development in my work, I think they miss the development of the refining of that texture and facture (or the opposite of refining it) in the sense that it is a consistent factor in the paintings flanking the garterbelt, calligraphic and collage periods.

I've often talked about my ability to draw, my facility, the thing that's always there, that I can count on. There's no question about the fact I'm a linear artist, a line man. Whereas some artists are colourists, others are what I call 'shapists' and still others are concerned with representation, volume, three-dimensional form, space and other non-twentieth century ideas. I'm working in the twentieth century. I'm aware of the reductivism in art and I reject it. One thing that's always been on my side is an interest in line, but I'm not a colourist (using the term in a traditional sense). Colour for me is not difficult however. From art school, when I had Harley Parker as a teacher, through to the publishing of the Itten book and then the later books by Albers and other writers on colour, I've always known those principles of simultaneous contrast, vibration and after-images and harmonies. For 25 years I've been aware of 'colour theory' and have been teaching it, but I will not let any 'theory' tell me what to do. Colour is for me an emotional concern and comes out of an emotional need.

I don't think I've ever had an image in my mind of a painting and how it would look before I painted it, in the way that, for instance, Michael Snow once said he had. I remember him telling me around '61 that he gets images on his mind, creates an image, and thinks about it – and while thinking about it, eliminates everything that is not important, ending up with the simplest possible statement he could make. (It was around the time he was doing paintings like *Drum, Book* and *Secret*

Shout). To me, it was an idea I'd never conceived of. Working in commercial art I had to come up with ideas for films, animation, commercial editorial art and so on. But when it comes to painting, the idea does not come first; it comes out of the painting process. I never ask 'what should I do a painting about?' Nor do I ask 'how?', nor 'why?' I just do it.

I see some things in the real world, which leave indelible images with me. Greg Curnoe does paintings about the Victoria Hospital which he sees from his window; I look out of my window and see the Toronto General Hospital, the Metropolitan United Church, the park, the winos, and the people sitting on benches and the cars going by, but very little of what's out there consciously ends up in my paintings. I don't think I've been interested yet in doing a painting of what I see out of my window, because I'm not really interested in representation. I love nature too much to mutilate it in copies.

When I sit here and look out of the window, I see unidentifiable forms in the leaf tonal patterns in the trees. I see lines, I see edges, I see abstraction. I don't see the trees to reproduce them the way they are. I see a pattern of grey-scale changes from black through to white; I see a tonal set-up. I see a very clear graphic image made from the tonal pattern that affects the various greens, from sap and leaf greens through to viridian and green-blue. The grey-scale tonal effect of parts in shadow, in half-shadow, and the parts that are being hit by brilliant sunlight, create a texture for me — a surface. I see two-dimensionally. Everything is surface, flat on a canvas.

I've always been interested in the look of dilapidation and age in the city, for instance in the area around Cabbagetown (before they built the developments of Moss Park and Regent's Park). This interest has to do with surface texture and the differences between old wood, new wood, concrete, asphalt, tar. I'm particularly interested in the scraping lines made by big trucks backing into alleyways, where there's brick on both sides and steel plates on the edges of the brick wall corners. I've taken photographs of this kind of subject matter and looked at it many times. When I've got nothing else to do, I like to walk around dilapidated areas because the images and the subject matter there, are the imagery and subject matter of New York City abstract expressionism. When I go to Alberta I miss the texture that surrounds me here in Toronto. People may wonder why I live downtown — how I

can stand the noise, the street cars. I couldn't stand living in a suburban area! There's absolutely nothing in a suburban area that would stimulate me to paint. I would probably end up being a magic or photo-realist because of that kind of environment. I like the dirty downtown environment because in all the subject matter — from broken windows stuffed with rags to windows with cardboard stained by the rain, to the look of scratched bricks, to painted grafitti — all of these images interest me. They interest me as artistic entities, rather than from the point of view that calls all this urban blight. Few critics realize that this is my concern, that I'm painting the same kind of subject matter the New York City abstract expressionists painted. They lived in New York City which was (and is) a dirty-looking city. It's that particular look that Robert Rauschenberg responds to. You can see it in Buffalo, in Thunder Bay, in Winnipeg, in any older city. You see incredible colour relationships as well as textural relationships. This has been really the subject matter of most of my abstractions since I lived on Wellesley Street between '60 and '62 and on Church Street since '65. It's a constant, consistent and continuing interest of mine which shows up in my work.

Another thing I really respond to is what happens to snow in the city. A day or so after a heavy snow fall, when the ploughs have cleared the streets, there are mountains of snow along the sidewalk, and the dirty, muddy slush splashes up onto those snow mountains and they begin to melt and disintegrate. I am fascinated by the sculptural forms caused by weathering and automobile splashing on these mounds of snow, particularly in March / April. Those paintings from '72 to '76 like *Lonely Sub Zero Sunday, Thoughts Drowning Feelings Ascending,* those gentle, dropped, textural paintings have a lot to do with my observations of the snowdrifts and snow patterns. I love the city, the dirty old city. Who are those people who call all the stuff I'm so interested in, urban blight? Who are those people who want the whole downtown area of Toronto to look like that around the Toronto Dominion Centre, Commerce Court, First Canadian Place? Nothing could be further from what I'm interested in than that area of downtown with its underground shopping malls.

A couple of works in my last show at Isaacs (painted between '72 and '76) are definitely subject matter based on this environment, between roughly Queen and King Street from Church to River Street. One in particular, the orange / yellow painting called *Prairie Dam No. 2,* although it has a similar composition to *Prairie Dam No. 1,* is actually based on the back of a truck. I love truck backs; they're like moving paintings. They're on the back of moving vans, on the back of large transports and I encounter them on the highway when I'm driving out West and back. I see them in the city. I love the look of peeling paint and the look of use and human spoilage of surfaces, especially the backs and sides of trucks.

Environment has a lot to do with what I paint, so I've produced different kinds of painting depending on the location of my various studios, the major ones being at Wellesley and Church, on Yonge at Bloor and at Church and Queen. Here, at Church and Queen, is where I have been living for eleven years and where I want to be.

The material in this catalogue has been taken from transcriptions of tapes of Dennis Burton talking about his work and taped interviews of Dennis Burton talking to Joan Murray about his work.

Tape 1. Burton – lecture at The Robert McLaughlin Gallery, 'Toronto in the '60s, the Artist's view', April 18, 1974
 2. Burton/Murray – April 23, 1976
 3. Burton/Murray – Sept. 7, 1976
 4. Burton/Murray – Sept. 7, 1976
 5. Burton/Murray – Nov. 1, 1976
 6. Burton – November 10, 11, 1976
 7. Burton – November 11, 1976
 8. Burton – November 11, 12, 1976
 9. Burton – November 13, 14, 1976
 10. Burton – November 15, 1976
 11. Burton – November 16, 1976

The Exhibition

2 Jeruvia 1956
  Oil on canvas
  24 x 30 in.
  Irving Grossman, Toronto

3 Monarch 1958
Oil on masonite
48 x 48 in.
The Isaacs Gallery, Toronto

4 Intimately Close-In 1958
Oil on masonite
48 x 48 in.
The National Gallery of Canada, Ottawa

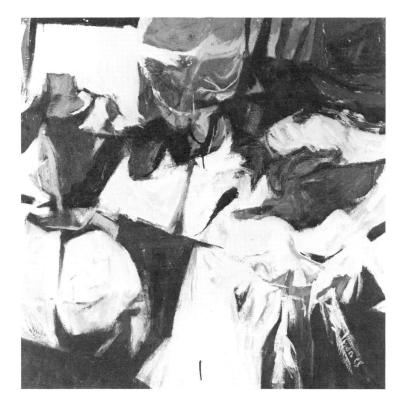

5 Serves Me Right (Anvil) 1959
Oil on masonite
48 x 60 in.
The Isaacs Gallery, Toronto

6 Drawing after **Intimately Close-In** 1960
Ink on paper
23 7/8 x 18 3/4 in.
Private collection, Montreal

7 Intimate 1960
Ink on paper
33 1/2 x 29 1/2 in.
The Isaacs Gallery, Toronto

8 Burlesque Case 1960
Oil on plywood
52 3/4 x 52 3/4 in.
The Isaacs Gallery, Toronto

9 Smokeshop Sex Marauder 1960
Oil and collage on masonite
48 x 60 in.
The Isaacs Gallery, Toronto

10 Drawing for **The Game of Life** 1960
Pencil on paper
9 x 11 5/16 in.
The National Gallery of Canada, Ottawa

11 Drawing for **The Game of Life** 1960
Oil on paper on board
15 x 15 in.
The Isaacs Gallery, Toronto

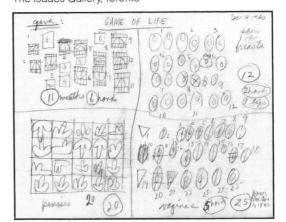

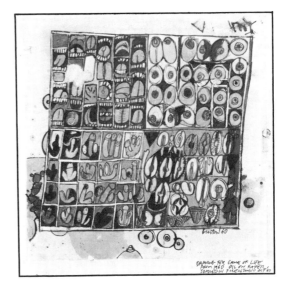

12 The Game of Life 1960
Oil on canvas
54 x 77 $^7/_8$ in.
The National Gallery of Canada, Ottawa

13 Brick of the Month – Neapolitan 1961
Oil on canvas
60 x 60 in.
Mrs. Gail Humphries, Kingston

14 False-True 1962
Oil on canvas
60 x 60 in.
Renée and David Perlmutter, Toronto

15 American Heroes and Foes 1963
Oil and collage on masonite
47 ⁷/₈ x 60 in.
Art Gallery of Ontario
Gift of Sam and Ayala Zacks, 1970

16 Silence 1963
Oil on canvas
60 x 60 in.
Mr. and Mrs. Martin Levene, Kitchener

17 Bay-Yonge-Bloor 1963
Oil on canvas
84 x 60 in.
Renée and David Perlmutter, Toronto

18 Room-Mates No. 3 1964-65
Oil and acrylic on canvas
60 x 60 in.
Gordon Sheppard, Montreal

19 Drawing for **Gate View Girl** 1965
Ink and wash on paper on cardboard
16 13/16 x 23 7/8 in.
Norman Mackenzie Art Gallery, Regina

20 **Gate View Girl** 1965
Oil on canvas
30 1/16 x 39 15/16 in.
Norman Mackenzie Art Gallery, Regina

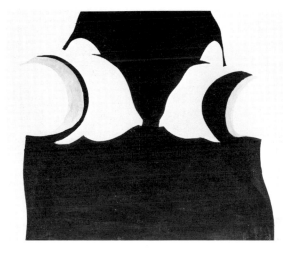

21 Mother, Earth, Love 1965
Oil and acrylic copolymer on canvas
60 x 80 in.
Art Gallery of Ontario
Gift from the Junior Women's Committee

22 Venus Evoked 1965
Oil on canvas
60 x 60 in.
Sir George Williams Art Galleries
Concordia University, Montreal

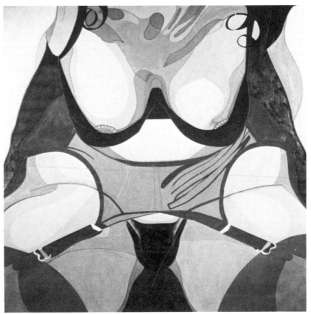

23 Girl 1966
Water colour and gouache on paper
15 3/4 x 12 5/8 in.
Judith and Tom Hendry, Toronto

24 Egypt Asleep 1966
Oil on canvas
60 x 60 1/8 in.
Walter Carsen, Toronto

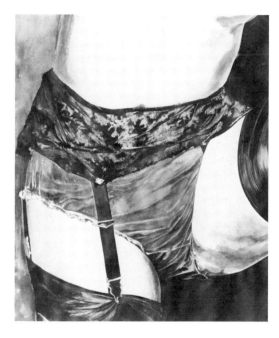

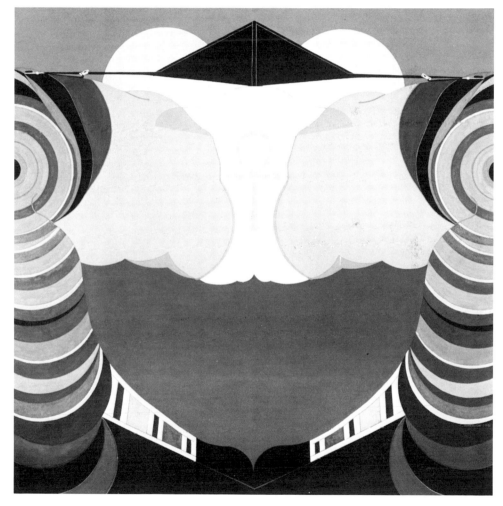

25 Mothers and Daughters 1966
Oil and acrylic copolymer on canvas
60 1/8 x 60 1/4 in.
The Robert McLaughlin Gallery
Purchase, 1976

26 Listening to the Stones 1966
Oil on canvas
60 x 60 in.
The Isaacs Gallery, Toronto

54

27 The Three Graces after Rubens 1967
Oil on canvas
60 x 60 in.
Dr. R.J. Shroyer, London

28 Yonique Metaphor – Prismadame 1967
Oil on canvas
60 x 60 in.
The Isaacs Gallery, Toronto

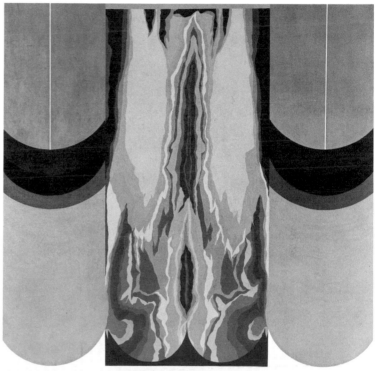

29 Niagara Rainbow Honeymoon No. 1 — The Bedroom 1967-68
Oil on canvas
60 x 60 in.
The Winnipeg Art Gallery
Donated by the Women's Committee, 1968

**30 Niagara Rainbow Honeymoon No. 4 — AUM —
The Sound of the Falls** 1968
Oil on canvas
60 x 60 in.
Mr. and Mrs. Lionel T. Brouse, Toronto

31 Rosedale Rebellion 1968
Oil on canvas
60 ¹/₈ x 60 ¹/₈ in.
The University of Western Ontario Permanent
Collection (Board of Governors Grant)

32 Greece and Egypt 1970
Ink and collage on cardboard on masonite
32 x 40 in.
The Isaacs Gallery, Toronto

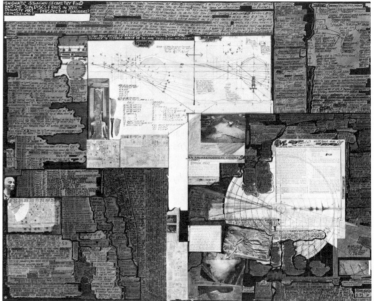

57

33 Seeaph 1971
Acrylic on canvas
64 x 82 in.
The Isaacs Gallery, Toronto

58

34 Concorde 1971
Acrylic on canvas
60 x 60 in.
The Isaacs Gallery, Toronto

35 A History and an Explanation of the Paintings 1972
Ink and collage on paper
21 x 16 1/2 in.
The Isaacs Gallery, Toronto

36 Locomotion 1972-73
Acrylic and oil glazes on canvas
72 x 80 in.
The Isaacs Gallery, Toronto

37 Drawing for **Up-Tight News** 1974
Ink on paper
12 x 12 3/4 in.
The Isaacs Gallery, Toronto

38 Up-Tight News 1974
Acrylic on canvas
64 1/8 x 47 1/8 in.
Indusmin Limited, Toronto

39 Bad Good Friday 1974-75
Acrylic on canvas
60 1/8 x 72 1/8 in.
The Robert McLaughlin Gallery
Purchase, 1976

40 Suspicion 1975
Acrylic and collage on canvas
60 x 72 in.
The Isaacs Gallery, Toronto

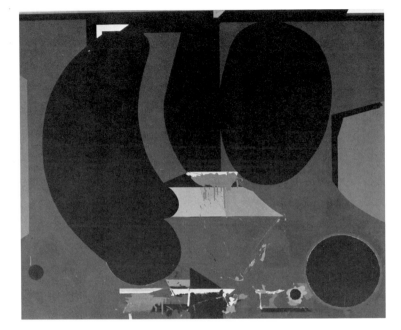

41 Big Prairie White Sky 1975
Acrylic and collage on canvas
54 x 84 in.
The Isaacs Gallery, Toronto

42 Coming Down 1976
Acrylic on canvas
72 x 90 in.
The Isaacs Gallery, Toronto

43 Nastaliq Automatique 1976
Acrylic on canvas
90 x 72 in.
The Isaacs Gallery, Toronto